Praise for *Super Agent*

"Joseph and JoAnn understand the heart and soul of real estate. Not only are their leadership and results in the business to be admired and respected, but their partnership both in marriage and in business is a treasured example for others. They are a true service to everyone they come in contact with. From the agent starting to grow to the agent with a huge team, *Super Agent* is a must read. They have taken the difficult, and with thought and care they've made it seem effortless."

— **Andrew and Mandi Monaghan**, The Monaghan Group,
Keller Williams Professional Partners

"JoAnn and Joseph Callaway have mastered how to run a thriving real estate business while remaining true to their principles and loved and admired by clients, colleagues, and competitors. *Super Agent* shares their techniques and guiding principles in a way that any agent can put into practice. Following their advice will help an agent give better service to clients and allow the business to grow successfully."

— **Michael J. Orr**, Director of the Center for
Real Estate Theory and Practice, W. P. Carey School of
Business at Arizona State University

"Once again, Those Callaways are true to form in *Super Agent*, a book I could not put down from cover to cover. All I ever needed to know to help real estate professionals take their business to the highest level is written in these pages. *Super Agent* is a true testament to real estate professionals sharpening the saw and becoming experts at their craft. The world of selling real estate has been forever changed."

— **Melissa M. Shapiro**, Senior Vice President,
Arizona State Manager, North American Title Company

"*Super Agent* is *the* brass tacks blueprint for creating a real estate business worth having. The new agent will find practical, down-to-earth ways to do that, but perhaps the bigger surprise is that the high-production agent will as well! We found ourselves reexamining our best practices, as this book exposed some gaps in our business and systems. Longtime agents in their pursuit of growth can so easily let old systems slip in favor of the latest idea. This book will put your compass back to True North."

—**Russell and Wendy Shaw**, GRI, CRS, Russell Shaw Group,
"Home of the No Hassle Listing," Realty One Group

"I simply could not put *Super Agent* down, and I have already ordered more copies for my friends in the industry. Joseph and JoAnn Callaway's second book by far exceeded my expectations. These two never disappoint. We are the third largest brokerage in the metropolitan Phoenix area, and we host a very successful coaching program. The coaching program provides one-on-one mentoring to both new and experienced agents, getting them to their true business potential in the least amount of time. *Super Agent* will now be the cornerstone of this training. The book provides an abundant amount of real estate business tactics, systems, and theories in an easy-to-comprehend manner. Every agent should read this book using a highlighter, as *Super Agent* will be the resource for your real estate business success. Do you want to succeed in real estate? Read *Super Agent*."

—**Heidi Zebro**, Vice President, DPR Realty, LLC

"These Super Agents care enough to share their highly successful secrets of unparalleled success and, most poignantly, of giving back. Those Callaways' sense of caring about each and every facet of home ownership and pride of community speaks to their uncanny success. If they reach more agents to do their utmost to fulfill their career expectations and the expectations of the community giving, they continue to pay it forward. Those Callaways demonstrate in their daily lives what it means to share, care, and give hope to each community they touch with their exuberance for real estate. They *are* the Super Agents of the past, present, and future. Those Callaways empower all of us to care more, to serve more, and to be more in our everyday careers and lives. And we thank them!"

—**Bill Rogers**, CEO and Founder, Homeowners Financial Group;
Co-founder, The Care Fund

"Brilliant in its simplicity and clarity, *Super Agent* is more than just the bible of success in the real estate business. It's a formula for success in any sales- and service-based organization. Joseph and JoAnn deliver Super Empowerment to all of their readers. This is a must-read for anyone serious about taking their business to the highest level!"

—**Dean Selvey**, Realtor with $1.2 billion in sales

"Wow! Super Job! As I read through *Super Agent*, each chapter is loaded with practical tips from real life, ready for agents to put to use to take their business to Super Agent status. Awesome. Destined to be another best seller!"

"*Super Agent* answers the questions, details the activities, and explains how to achieve a super level of performance. I can't wait to share it with my agents, both new and experienced. I certainly expect to see super results from those who follow this book's advice."

"Is *Super Agent* a how-to book or a motivational manual? Either way, it's outstanding. From real-life examples to implementation strategies, it covers everything from the basics to the subtle touches that mean so much. I loved the client follow-up discussions with the real-life example of 100+ referrals from one client. I've seen so many agents utilize the 'one and done' mentality toward a buyer or seller, but providing top-notch client service and creating that client for life will pay off for the Super Agent."

"As a broker, I loved the discussion about working with another agent in a cross sale. Whether you're helping a new agent or showing your listing for another agent, the sooner you start building the relationship, the sooner the next cross sale with that agent will occur. Oh, and I appreciated the section on communication from the client's perspective. The importance of staying in touch with a phone call or other means of correspondence cannot be overstated. Outstanding!"

"Apparently, I am quoted in Chapter 4 about 'practicing safe real estate.' Those Callaways' follow-up about risk reduction, knowing the contract, and being prepared will make brokers around the country smile and thank them immensely. I wish those Callaways the best success with their new book. And stay hungry!"

—**Jim Sexton**, Designated Broker, Realty One Group

"Most people who obtain a real estate license have a wonderful goal to help people experience success in buying or selling their home. Unfortunately, not everyone has been taught how to make that goal a reality, until now. Joseph and JoAnn Callaway have done just that with their new book, *Super Agent*. There is no longer any guesswork. This book lays out a clear path with everything a committed professional must do to build a truly professional real estate practice. This is not theory; they are sharing from their own experience. All you need to do is read it, study it, think it, and do it. You'll be glad you did."

—**Steve Chader**, Broker Owner, Keller Williams Integrity First Realty

"*Super Agent* will become the bible for all real estate agents, whether brand-new or veteran. It is a step-by-step guide filled with wit and wisdom on how to go from an ordinary to an extraordinary real estate agent. Joseph and JoAnn Callaway are true leaders in the industry who practice their craft every day. *Caution!* Read this book only if you are ready for massive success!"

—**Kirsten and Doug Hill**, Associate Brokers, The Hill Group,
Coldwell Banker Residential Brokerage,
2013 Top Producers in Arizona for Coldwell Banker

"I loved Those Callaways' first book, *Clients First*, and was not sure how they were going to be able to top it, but they did. *Super Agent* is an easy-to-read how-to book. Reading this book, I was amazed at how these sales practices could be used not only by Realtors but also by any person wanting to succeed in any career. *Super Agent* is a book that can be used by any sales professional, whether you are a Realtor, mortgage lender, insurance agent, title representative, car salesperson, or even a doctor. We are all in the business of building and maintaining relationships. Joseph and JoAnn have earned the right to write these books."

—**Delia A. Wilkens**, Senior Mortgage Consultant, Guild Mortgage Company, 2013
President of the Hispanic Association of Real Estate Professionals of NAHREP

"Beyond a doubt, this is a book that every real estate agent should own. *Super Agent* is the best and most comprehensive book I've read on what to do, how to do it, and why. Those Callaways share where to find buyers and sellers and how to work with them, what activities are most productive, budgeting ideas and allocation of funds when building a business, building your team/staff, the necessity of strong affiliate relationship, loyalty considerations, social media and advertising that work, developing an unbelievably strong referral network, and so much more. This will take you from A to Z in all areas, whether you are a new agent or a 20-year veteran wanting to become even better. Invest in yourself with the outstanding book."

—**Marge Lindsay**, CRB, CRS, CRI, CRMS, Director of Education, Associate Broker, West USA Realty; Past President of the Arizona Association of Realtors

"This book is a must read for the entire real estate industry—agents, lenders, bankers, title companies, home warranty representatives, and any other vendors who serve buyers and sellers. *Clients First* left many people thirsty for the applications and specific steps to create a multimillion-dollar real estate business—*Super Agent* will quench your thirst! This book is filled with golden nuggets. This is one of those books you will want to use as a reference guide to build the real estate business of your dreams and become a top producer! Every new professional in our industry will be set up for success if they apply the 5 Super Powers."

—**Michelle Schwartz**, Executive Vice President, Old Republic Title

"I'm reading Joseph and JoAnn Callaway's new book *Super Agent*, and I realize that after 10 years of my own real estate career, I am one of those agents who have been so distracted over the years by the next 'shiny object.' *Super Agent* lays out for you all you need to focus on without becoming distracted. Joseph and JoAnn provide principles to follow that will yield you the result you need to become the Super Agent that they themselves are today, with over $1 billion in sales in 10 years. I wish they had written this book 10 years ago because, as they say after each chapter, 'You can do this!' And you know what? After 10 years in the business and reading this book, I am now saying, 'Yes I can!'"

—**Richie Laser**, Realtor, President, and CEO, Follow Up Results

"*Super Agent* is a blueprint that takes away any guesswork. It is the most thought-out real estate business model I have seen. It's broken down into systems, models, and concepts. If any agent currently in real estate wants to reach the highest level in a professional real estate career, then I strongly recommend reading *Super Agent*. Joseph and JoAnn will take you to places you never dreamed of."

—**Grey Sehnert**, Realtor, 2012 President of NAHREP Arizona; President of Project Maryvale

"With *Super Agent*, Those Callaways have done it again! There have been less than a handful of amazing books on creating and sustaining an effective and extremely profitable real estate business. This is a one-of-a-kind masterpiece on that very subject. They have combined old-fashioned and sometimes abandoned concepts along with today's revolutionary ideas to create the best how-to book ever! I am a fan for life."

—**Rick Geha**, Keller Williams Mega Agent and Owner

"Brilliant! Finally, real estate now has a comprehensive book written by practitioners who excel at the highest levels of our profession every day. They do it with style, grace, and humility. They are fiercely loyal to their clients and always put them first. This book gives the 'ordinary' agent a definitive plan to be a Super Agent. Those Callaways have shown that this is not pie-in-the-sky thinking. It is very realistic, and this is the blueprint for success. This is the best book for the industry since *The Millionaire Real Estate Agent*. It should be mandatory reading for anyone looking to be a success in residential real estate sales."

—**Jeff Sutherlin**, Broker Owner, United Brokers Group

"What an amazing book. This was put together so logically and with easy-to-follow, step-by-step information with examples and definitions. I started reading and the next thing I knew, I was highlighting and my book was completely highlighted because so many things struck a chord with me. I started taking notes on the side and then had to get a special notebook so I could write longer notes. I really started looking at this book as more than a casual read but a complete study guide, an advanced degree in real estate! It was something I thought would be a casual book to read at the coffee shop, but then I realized I needed to be someplace that I could really focus and study all the principles. Everything written in this book is essential. As I was going through the book, I also realized that so many examples given apply to almost everyone in business. Whether it is putting clients first or detaching yourself from the outcome, we live this world every day. These examples and guidelines we can apply to everything we do during the day, whether you're a teacher, dentist, lawyer, parent, or CEO. We all have customers in one way or another, and many of these principles we can apply to each circumstance."

"This book applies to new agents or experienced agents. As a new agent or someone looking to get into the business, some books suggest doing things that I might find a little difficult because it just would not be me. They would offer marketing and selling suggestions that just wouldn't work with my personality or comfort level. This book allows you to be yourself—which is someone who wants to be a Super Agent by helping others in a very emotional experience. Be a Super Agent by focusing on your client, knowledge base, and caring for all involved, doing your job fully and responsibly."

"I love this business! It has given me a completely different viewpoint. I feel proud to be in the real estate business, and I want to grow to become a *Super Agent*!"

—**Connie Sana**, *The Arizona Republic*

"After decades of teaching, training, motivating, and supervising great Realtors, it is refreshing and delightful to read a step-by-step manual recounting how Those Callaways built an extraordinary business from humble beginnings. This is a guide for the beginner, for the Realtor at the tipping point of one's career, and for the team evolving into a Super Team. *Super Agent* guides agents to believe, to decide, and to do the things that put the *Clients First* and grow their business organically. This is a must read for real estate agents at any stage of their growth in business. It is fun, interesting, and really an instructive guide."

—**John Foltz**, MBA, CRB, Vice President, Homeowners Financial Group,
The Care Fund Chairman, Realtor of the Year for 2010,
Past President of the Arizona Association of Realtors

"I've been coaching agents for over 10 years, and when I started reading *Super Agent*, I couldn't put it down. The one common question I get from new agents is, 'Is there a book that will give me the ins and outs of how to become successful in real estate?' and now I can answer 'Yes.' *Super Agent* is a cookbook with recipes to provide an honest and basic approach to how Realtors should work to become successful in their real estate careers. It will be at the top of my recommended reading list to all agents, both new and experienced."

—**Deanna Bone**, Associate Broker and Director for DPR Success Coaching

"It is all I can do to not mark up this copy of *Super Agent* with a billion different colored highlighters. I love the notion that we don't have to assume some predetermined character set to become a real estate agent; rather, we can draw out from within ourselves the qualities, honesty, and individuality that already *is* a real estate agent! That really rocks! I am going back and reading it word for word, taking it all in."

—**Billie "BK" Thornton**, (new) Realtor, DPR Realty, Arizona

Praise for *Clients First*

"This book really hits home with me. I've always said that legendary customer service shouldn't be rocket science. If you treat your clients well, they will become raving fans. They'll come back again and again, they'll sing your praises to their friends, and your sales will multiply. Joseph and JoAnn Callaway get it—and their Clients First philosophy is the reason for their fabulous success. Read *Clients First*, learn from Those Callaways, and watch your business grow."

—**Ken Blanchard**, coauthor of
The One Minute Manager and *Great Leaders Grow*

"JoAnn and Joseph have put together practical and powerful real-world information that's going to help you think about your business, your customers, and your life differently. I'd recommend this book to anybody who wants to build a great business and great relationships and live a great life."

—**Brian Buffini**, coauthor of
Work by Referral: Live the Good Life!; Chairman and
Founder of Buffini & Company, leading training
and coaching company in North America

"Albert Einstein once said, 'It is high time that the ideal of success should be replaced by the ideal of service.' In *Clients First*, JoAnn and Joseph Callaway not only demonstrate how living the ideal of service has created the great success in their lives but also share how you can apply it to create success in your own life. Along the way, you will be entranced by their love story for each other as well as for their clients."

—**Sharon Lechter**, coauthor of
Rich Dad series books, *Three Feet from Gold*, and *Outwitting the Devil*

"This wonderful book gives your proven, step-by-step processes to build wonderful client relationships, keep clients coming back, and give you an endless chain of good referrals."

—**Brian Tracy**, author of
The Power of Self-Confidence

"I've been a 'competing broker' in JoAnn and Joseph Callaway's market for several years. I wish all of the competition was like this—willing to share and help others grow. They make our industry a better place. Read this book."

—**Jay Thompson**, Founder of
PhoenixRealEstateGuy.com and Zillow Director
of Industry Outreach & Social Media

"If you look upon the title of this book not as two words but as one omnipotent idea, and then live by that idea, you'll be doing what this wonderful book wants you to do."

—**Jay Conrad Levinson**, the Father of
Guerrilla Marketing and author of the *Guerrilla Marketing* series

"In their remarkable new business book, *Clients First*, Joseph and JoAnn Callaway clearly and precisely answer the often-asked question, 'What is the secret to your incredible success?' Knowing that in real estate, just as in so many other industries, that there is really no 'secret' to success, JoAnn and Joseph nonetheless explain the three keys that have led to their extraordinary success in selling over 4,000 homes since 1997. Their two-word mission statement, 'Clients First,' encapsulates so much more of what it takes to succeed than one can imagine. But it is far from a simplistic look at the steps it takes to succeed; rather, it is an honest, in-depth reflection of what it took for them to become so wildly successful despite being unassuming and unpretentious 'typical' Americans, and how anyone can apply the lessons learned in their book to replicate their success."

—**Lynn Effinger**, author of
Believe to Achieve

"*Clients First* is a deeply personal story about the true meaning of uplifting service. This book is proof positive that service can be your sustainable strategy for success."

—**Ron Kaufman**, *New York Times* best-selling author of
*Uplifting Service: The Proven Path to Delighting Your Customers, Colleagues,
and Everyone Else You Meet*

SUPER AGENT

Other books by Joseph and JoAnn Callaway

Clients First, the Two Word Miracle

SUPER AGENT

REAL ESTATE SUCCESS
AT THE HIGHEST LEVEL

Joseph & JoAnn Callaway

WILEY

Cover image: Aaron Blackburn
Cover design: Aaron Blackburn

Published by John Wiley & Sons, Inc., Hoboken, New Jersey
Published simultaneously in Canada

Limit of Liability/Disclaimer of Warranty: While the publisher and author have used their best efforts in
preparing this book, they make no representations or warranties with the respect to the accuracy or
completeness of the contents of this book and specifically disclaim any implied warranties of
merchantability or fitness for a particular purpose. No warranty may be created or extended by sales
representatives or written sales materials. The advice and strategies contained herein may not be suitable
for your situation. You should consult with a professional where appropriate. Neither the publisher nor the
author shall be liable for damages arising herefrom.

For general information about our other products and services, please contact our Customer Care
Department within the United States at (800) 762-2974, outside the United States at (317) 572-3993 or
fax (317) 572-4002.

Wiley publishes in a variety of print and electronic formats and by print-on-demand. Some material
included with standard print versions of this book may not be included in e-books or in print-on-demand.
If this book refers to media such as a CD or DVD that is not included in the version you purchased, you
may download this material at http://booksupport.wiley.com. For more information about Wiley products,
visit www.wiley.com.

ISBN 978-1118-83425-1 (paper); ISBN 978-1-118-89171-1 (ebk);
ISBN 978-1-118-89179-7 (ebk)

Printed in the United States of America
10 9 8 7 6 5 4 3 2 1

This book is dedicated to all our fellow agents. A super agent lives in each of you.

Contents

Acknowledgments

We wish to express our gratitude to our real estate profession for the opportunity to succeed beyond our dreams. Thank you to every client, every agent, every vendor, and every affiliate to whom we owe so much. We wake up feeling grateful every day.

A special thank-you to Marge Lindsay, Michelle Schwartz, Heidi Zebro, and Gail Buck. You have all been there for the journey.

Thank you to our family and our team. No one succeeds alone.

Finally, we wish to thank our editor, Richard Narramore, without whom this book would never have happened.

Authors' Note

When we met, it was love at first sight. Only later did we learn that we shared a love for books. JoAnn said that she had read the entire Encyclopedia Britannica by the age of 10. I told her about getting special permission to check out books from the adult section of the public library when I was seven years old. Our conversations during our marriage have been richer for it.

Over the years, we've shared countless reads. We read James Michener's *Space* and Herman Wouk's *The Winds of War* and *War and Remembrance* aloud to each other. I introduced JoAnn to John D. MacDonald's Travis McGee, and she gave me *Shanna* by Kathleen E. Woodiwiss. Today, she has her favorites and I have mine.

Every night, JoAnn reads three newspapers.

Years ago, we dreamed of writing books, and proceeded to put together a collection of reference books on the subject of writing. We've owned hundreds of dictionaries, style books, and how-to guides compiled and composed by literary agents, editors, publishers, writers, and writing instructors. This collection has grown and contracted several times during our marriage as we've swung from buying sprees to purging resolutions each New Year's. Few volumes have survived except the books on writing by writers.

These are the treasures, the jewels that we will never part with. We have *Bird by Bird* by Anne Lamott, *Writing Down the Bones* by Natalie Goldberg, and Stephen King's small volume titled *On Writing*. In his book, King imparts the story of his career and then gives his advice on how to write. It is from this one handbook we draw so much.

As we entered the real estate profession, we naturally gravitated to the business section of our local bookstore, where we purchased book after book. We have books on leadership and accounting, as well as biographies of tycoons and business leaders. We have all the *Rich Dad, Poor Dad* issues. When it comes to real estate, we would presume to claim that every book on the subject published over the past 16 years has transited our shelves, and we have even picked up earlier publications in used book stores.

When our editor at John Wiley & Sons suggested a real estate agent's bible, we thought back to all those books on writing and how few were actually by writers. As we survey the scene, we see so many fine books on selling real estate but few by active agents working every day with clients.

It is our sincere hope that this modest offering of *Super Agent* will become your Stephen King's *On Writing*, and that it will bring you joy.

Be a Super Agent

"Be all you can be."

—U.S. Army slogan

"We are what we repeatedly do. Excellence, therefore, is not an act, but a habit."

—Aristotle

"First, be a good agent."

—Chapter 4, page 33, *Super Agent*

1 Who Wants to Be a Super Agent?

Who wouldn't want to be a super agent? Super agents make more money, have the respect of their peers, the gratitude of their clients and they work less hours. How do we know? We know because we are super agents. JoAnn and I have been licensed for 17 years and have sold over one and a half billion dollars' worth of homes. We say this only because it is important for you to know such things are possible. Had we only known in the beginning how incredible this profession can be, it would have saved us so much time, doubt, and angst. We are currently active in the business and continue to serve our clients every day.

Super Rewards

How many super agents are there and how much money do they make? Let's first define super income. The national average income for real estate agents is currently around $45,000 per year, so let's say a super agent is someone who makes twice the average. Yes, agent averages vary from Mayberry to Manhattan but the two-to-one relationship is the point. If you are making double the average for your area, you are doing well. We'll get to the specifics but let me say there are thousands upon thousands of agents who make a six-figure income today, and the upper limits are in the mid-to-high seven figures. Yes, we are talking millions here. JoAnn and I earned over $6 million in our best year and our best month was just short of a million dollars' gross commission income. Again, we only tell you this because as you come to know us in these pages you will realize how unlikely our success has been and how likely it is that you can do as well or better than us.

The rewards that put the super in super agents, however, are often not measured in money. Vendors, fellow professionals, and clients all respect super agents because a super agent does more business, which creates opportunities to serve more clients—that is where the real reward comes. There is no greater satisfaction than closing a transaction and having the client thank you for a job well done. We help clients through one of the biggest moments in their lives and knowing we did it well fills our hearts.

In case you missed it, we said super agents work less hours. That's correct and sometimes much less. There are many super agents who have achieved such a degree of ownership in their business that the time they labor is spent working on the business, not in the business. Because these agents work on their business, they are able to see the forest for the trees. They are able to innovate and improve. They come up with better ways to get and serve clients. They take weekends off. They take extended weekends. They take vacations. They do all this because they have time to think and that time is the best time you can spend.

Super Profession

So, who wouldn't want to be a super agent? For that matter, who wouldn't want to be a real estate agent? Ours is a wonderful profession for several reasons but let's start with opportunity. Anyone who passes the state test can be a real estate agent. A member of our extended family holds the title. She took the Arizona Real Estate Exam 12 times! We don't tell you this to embarrass her. We tell you this out of pride. Her eighth-grade teacher told us she didn't think this girl would graduate high school. But she didn't let that hold her back. She worked harder than everybody else and graduated. Then she went on to college and got her two-year degree. Then she got a real estate license. Now, at 30-plus, she is just finishing her last classes for a four-year degree. If that girl, whose teacher doubted her future, can be an agent, you can, too.

JoAnn and I know thousands of agents and they are all so different. Real estate is not the Rockettes, all weighing within a pound of each other. What they all have in common is that they have little in common. The best you can say about how they succeed is that there is no one way to succeed. Agents come in all shapes and sizes. They have various talents and some have no talents. They come from all sorts of backgrounds, and only a few could be described as attractive. They are from many cultures and some speak poor English. These are newly arrived to the United States from Southeast Asia or Eastern Europe or some other country of origin and most started with little or no money. They do not operate the same way or practice the same specialty. Our profession led the way in equal opportunity home ownership. Our profession is open to all who ask.

Super Opportunity

The purest form of opportunity is commission income. We are not held back by hierarchy or ceilings or time on the job. Commission is the closest thing we have to a free market. We are free to negotiate commission and we are free to not negotiate. We are free to earn it or not earn it. How much we make, how we make it, and when we make it is up to us. This is opportunity.

Just think about this. We do not need to purchase and maintain an inventory. We get to sell a tangible item without having to buy, build, or produce it. We don't even have to list it for sale. We can simply bring a buyer and earn a commission. Don't tell this to the manufacturers or the retailers. Let's keep this as our little secret. Being a real estate agent is the greatest thing since sliced bread.

For many, one of the early attractions to our profession is the low level of entry requirements. Some jurisdictions have raised standards but most states require anywhere from 50 to 150 hours of classes followed by passing a test. The financial requirements are usually less than $1,000, including school tuition and association fees. Some brokers will even offset a portion of these costs. The time required can be measured in weeks. If you are in a hurry, you can decide to enter the real estate profession one day and only a month later be handing out business cards.

A newly minted agent has many options to succeed. Most brokers offer excellent training and want new agents to do well. Many senior agents give back by mentoring new agents. Wonderful coaches are available. Seminars, conferences, and conventions are plentiful on the calendar. All considered, why do we even ask the question who wants to be a real estate agent, much less a super agent?

Dismal Statistics

Statistics paint a much different picture. The numbers tell us that the average new real estate agent is in and out of the business in less than five years. They earn very little and if they are lucky they sell two or three homes to family or friends before the lack of income drives them to do something else.

For the agents who do make it, the picture is not much better. The average career for an agent is 11 to 13 years and their median income is under $50,000 per year before expenses. The average agent sells ten homes per year. This is a dismal picture often drawn by statisticians, self-appointed experts, well-meaning naysayers, and those who would have us all averaged down to mediocrity.

Our first exposure to real estate was billed as an opportunity night at the local real estate school. JoAnn and I attended and the elderly gentleman conducting the session gave a similar statistical description of the business and it was another 15 years before I could talk JoAnn into getting a license. He did mention that some agents were very successful but by then we were 45 minutes into his talk and JoAnn was rolling her eyes. We left with JoAnn telling me how stupid the whole real estate license idea was and that she believed that the old guy never met a successful real estate agent in his life. I offered some sort of lame response but I might as well have been defending violence in movies. We had one of our lively discussions all the way home. The fact is we had no idea as to how successful a real estate agent can be and we went on to other endeavors, delaying our success for a decade and a half.

Let's talk about statistics for a minute. A comic once said, "63 percent of statistics are made up on the spot." Then he said, "No, maybe it's 58 percent." The point is that statistics suffer a great deal of abuse and they should not influence you. Mark Twain said, "There are lies, there are damn lies, and there are statistics." Don't lose the next 15 years like we did. I am here to tell you that super agents exist and you can be one of them.

Don't Be Held Back

What are the characteristics of super agents, what makes them tick, and how can you become one? We'll come to that, but first let's talk about what else, beside statistics, can hold you back. Notice that no mention has been made of good looks, youth, sales talent since birth, a fancy wardrobe, a big car, or rich friends. These don't matter but a person with negative beliefs will say they do. A negative person will say, "But I don't have savings to last six months before I start earning commissions." This is because some other negative believer didn't make a sale for their first six months in the business. Let me tell you this business is so incredible that on any given day, you can get up in the morning, hold an open house, meet a client, write a contract, and open escrow before the sun goes down. You might have to wait 30 days for your money but our first sale in this business was a cash deal that closed in five days.

We could go on to list all the negative statements and beliefs that hold agents back but then this book would weigh five pounds. People fail. They fail and they give up. They fail and they seek company so they help others fail by passing on negative thoughts. But super agents succeed because they don't listen to the statistics and the failures who want companionship. Super agents believe they can make it. Do they never fail? Far from it. Super agents fail every day, every hour, every minute. Do you think the open house described above was a cakewalk? No, it was filled with looky-loos and travelers trying to decide between your state and the one 300 miles away. But the super agent knew for every failure they were one step closer to success. Every failure is an opportunity to learn from our mistakes. It's not the one who falls down who matters, it is the one who gets back up who wins.

If you have negative thoughts or beliefs that hold you back, you should probably work on purging them rather than search for a line of work where they don't matter. Truth is there are plenty of jobs out there where you can be negative and still earn a living. You won't rise to the top but you can get by. These are jobs where you sell your life for wages. If you stay in school long enough and earn a high enough degree you might even merit a decent salary. Still, in these scenarios, you will be one of the negative ones, the first to be laid off and the last to be hired.

In a commission-opportunity environment, negative thoughts and beliefs have no place. Super agents are positive they can succeed. They believe they will succeed and while the road may be littered with obstacles they are not going to be one of them.

The Three *D's*

What does go on in the mind of a super agent? What are the common traits or characteristics that set them apart? JoAnn and I know many super agents. We have spoken to audiences all over the country and in these travels we've had lunch or dinner with market-leading agents in many cities. We belong to two separate mastermind groups of 20 top agents each. We meet monthly over lunch to discuss issues in our market.

We know the master coaches and we have conducted our own version of research over the years in an effort to define the field and ourselves. What makes super agents tick? What makes us tick? Although, we could wax on about a hundred forgettable traits, We've narrowed it down to the three *D's*. Super agents are decided. Super agents are driven. And super agents are determined.

Decision

Deciding is where everything begins. You decide to buy a new car before you go shopping. Then the work begins. You have to figure out if you can afford a new car. You have to get your credit up to snuff. You have to clean up your trade-in. You have to go shopping and endure the negotiation process.

Every super agent we know decides. They decide to grow. They decide to hold. They decide to go in a new direction or they decide to stay the course. Everything they do, they do on purpose.

Two years into our careers, we decided to double our income and two years later we did. There was work involved in between but we would have worked during that two years anyway. The key was that we decided first and the result followed. After that, we decided to double the business again and we did. We are now in a recovering market, so we decided recently to double our business once more and this year we are up 50 percent. How much of that is the improving market and how much is the decision, we do not know. We do know plenty of agents who are experiencing no improvement in business because they have simply not yet decided that the recovery is real.

The decision comes first. If you want to be a super agent, do not drift along in the river of life. Decide and the result will follow. Can you decide? Of course you can. You decide everyday, all day long. Life is one long series of choices and you decide on each one. If you want to be a super agent, simply make the decision and then make sure all the decisions that follow are consistent with your first one. That is the beauty and secret of success. You don't have to make a big move. Success is the culmination of all the little moves, the small choices, the little decisions you make each day. You can do that.

Drive

What is drive anyway? Is it like art and you just know it when you see it or is it in some way definable? We've heard drive described as motivation but motivation comes and goes and drive is so much more constant. Is it ego? Perhaps. But to be healthy it must be a controlled ego. An uncontrolled ego is arrogance and we have yet to meet a true super agent who is arrogant. In fact, a common thread among the high achievers seems to be humility and gratitude. We often just can't believe it was that easy. We decided, we worked for it, and we got what we asked for.

Is drive a capacity for work? Most super agents can easily work a 16-hour day and get up the next morning to do it again. But when we get the opportunity to work less, we take it.

We believe drive is wanting what you decide on. Drive is obsession with what you decide you want. Drive goes beyond belief in your goals. Drive is seeing those goals as a reality. Drive is sureness and yes, drive is something you recognize when you see it.

Can you be driven? Of course you can. Remember that puppy you wanted when you were a child? Remember your first crush? Drive is within all of us. To be driven you must simply set yourself free to want again. Be a child without all the limitations put upon you as you grew up. You can do that.

Determination

Finally comes determination. Super agents are determined to keep going no matter what obstacles or setbacks beset them. Super agents are stubborn. Calvin Coolidge, our 30th president put it this way. "Nothing in the world can take the place of persistence. Talent will not; nothing is more common than unsuccessful men with talent. Genius will not; unrewarded genius is almost a proverb. Education will not; the world is full of educated derelicts. Persistence and determination alone are omnipotent. The slogan "Press On" has solved and always will solve the problems of the human race." This quote sits on JoAnn's desk. She looks at it everyday. She has had occasion to read it to a number of people who needed to hear it. Another quote on her desk is stamped into a metal paperweight. They are the last words Churchill said to the British people as German bombs fell on London: "Never, never, never give up."

Heroes never give up. No matter what the odds or how many times they are told they cannot win, heroes keep going. Marathon runners, who finish, do not give up. Super agents do not give up.

We've all given up at one time or the other. Just look back on your regrets. We all have them and they were all a form of giving up. Oh, we excused them at the time. We rationalized how this was for the best. Since JoAnn and I entered the real estate profession, we have not given up. We have not given up on our dreams, our clients, or our decisions. We have no regrets.

Can you do this? Can you decide? Can you be driven? Can you not give up? Of course you can. Becoming a super agent is within your reach. It is yours for the asking. Who wants to be a super agent? You do.

Chapter 1 Summary

Super Agents Experience Super Rewards

- High income.
- Respect and satisfaction.
- Less hours.

Real Estate Is a Super Profession

- Easy entry.
- Opportunity.
- Open to all.

Don't Be Held Back

- Dismal statistics.
- Negative beliefs.
- Failure.

The Three *D's*

- Super agents are decided.
- Super agents are driven.
- Super agents are determined.

The Five Super Powers of a Super Agent

Not all real estate agents have super powers, but those who do have long and rewarding careers.

The First Super Power

We began as terrible agents. We were halfway through life and broke. We rented our house, leased our car, and owed my dad money. We got licensed and thought it meant we could do anything. Everything we did was about the commission, the money. We thought we could control others when we could barely control ourselves. We were a danger to our clients and our profession. Then we changed.

Our first super power came as they do, in a moment of realization. The clouds parted, lightning struck. Not really, but looking back it seemed that way. JoAnn and I were well on our way to losing our licenses. We had already had two commission-ectomies. That's where you pay for your mistakes with part of your commission at closing. The first house was on septic and we had it listed on sewer. The second was 300 square feet smaller than we said on the listing. Then it happened.

We had this lady who had found her dream home and wanted it so badly she and her husband asked that we write an offer contingent on selling their house. That meant we had to hustle. During the first hour of the first open house a couple walked in with no agent and said this was the wife's dream home and if they could just buy it, we could list their house. This would mean four commissions to us and we wrote an offer. That's when the trouble began.

The problem was that it was a low offer because it was more than the Buyers could afford and that meant the Sellers would have to settle for less than they needed. We began the negotiations, going back and forth with counteroffer after counteroffer.

We were in the car with counter-number seven when JoAnn said, "Maybe we should undo this deal?" I managed to not wreck the car and asked her what she meant. She said, "This is not a good deal for the Seller, they need more money than this for the next house, and it is not a good deal for the Buyers, because it's more than they can afford. All that matters is that we do the right thing and keep the clients." This was a new concept for me. We were only $5,000 apart and there was a lot of commission at stake. We could lose both clients and have nothing. But I said yes.

We went to the Sellers and told them what we thought and promised that we would get them another buyer. We took the rejected counter to the Buyers and promised that we would find them another dream home they could afford. Then we went home.

The next morning we were changed. We could no longer just tell our clients what they wanted to hear. We couldn't just put the right spin on what we said. We had to trust the truth and that was the first key: Honesty. From that morning on we had to know what we were doing. No more commission-ectomies. This was our second key: Competence. From that moment forward it could not be all about us, it became all about the clients, and we had our third key: Care. This was our first super power, the power to put the client first.

This one realization transformed our lives and our practice. Our business went viral as the clients we put first sent us their family and friends and then those clients sent their referrals. It truly was faster than a speeding bullet.

This was 1997, in Scottsdale, Arizona, with everyone and their brother holding a real estate license. One agent joked at a seminar, "I went to the supermarket last night and ran into three real estate agents. One was working produce and another checked me out." Interest rates were over 8 percent and there were so many houses on the market it took an average of 152 days to sell.

In spite of all that, JoAnn and I, operating as Those Callaways, sold over $30 million worth of homes, more than 150 transactions in our first full calendar year. All we did and all we knew was that we had to put our clients first. We had a super power and we exercised it every day.

This super power can be yours for the claiming. Simply say, "Yes." Make the commitment to put your clients first and then speak that commitment until it becomes ingrained. When life challenges your commitment, you must keep it against all temptations. Remember the three keys—Honesty, Competence, and Care—and work toward holding all three whole and complete. Not just two keys and most of the third, but all of them because it is in their completeness that *Clients First* becomes a super power.

The Second Super Power

Years and years ago, I worked in a large company and there were two goofballs, Bob and Tim, who loaded trucks in the warehouse and every time they screwed something up they blamed it on poor communication. Over the years I've observed hundreds of Bobs and hundreds of Tims with the same complaint. Because these guys were such error magnets, I gave communication short shift. I thought it was just an excuse. If they had just cared, they would have asked. They would have found out. Why put the blame on the company's communication? I was wrong. Not about Bob and Tim. They were ne'er-do-wells and are probably out there somewhere today, complaining about not being told something, as if the world owed them an explanation to all things, including why they are no further along than when I first knew them. But I was wrong about communication.

Understanding the importance of communication is a super power you can have for the asking. All that is required is that you understand the basic human need for information. As a life form we crave information. When CNN announced it was going to broadcast all news, all the time, 24 hours a day, the critics said it wouldn't fly. Today, there are dozens, if not hundreds, of news channels worldwide. The Internet is totally about delivering information. We are curious. We seek to know, and yes, we are hopeless gossips. We are human.

Solitary confinement is considered a terrible punishment because it denies us knowledge of our surroundings. We anguish, we worry, we imagine possibilities in the absence of hard data. Then an agent says to me that their client went crazy during a transaction and I don't wonder why because that same agent never answers their phone, never returns calls, and then blames problem issues on lack of communication just like Bob and Tim.

If you care, if you put your client first, you will understand your client's need for information and you will become a super communicator.

When you conduct real estate business every day the basics become second nature.

You quote contract clauses like cereal-box labels and you begin to assume everyone has the same casual understanding of the complexities of a real estate transaction as you do. A super agent knows differently. A super agent never forgets the first time they heard escrow explained and a super agent keeps her clients informed and comfortable with the process.

JoAnn has a couple of rules she lives by. Let's start with the phone. JoAnn figures it is easier to take a call than return one. She believes a phone conversation, in addition to being personal, gets more done, in less time than any other form of communication short of a face-to-face conversation, and she has plenty of those. She has one rule for herself and everyone else at Those Callaways, and that is you don't go home at night until every call is returned. JoAnn uses e-mail because it is a faster way to deliver written correspondence but when she wants to make a point or make someone feel special she sends snail mail and some of that is handwritten. She uses text messaging as another form of conversation without having to wait to get with someone. She tries to match the communication channel to the recipients preferred method.

JoAnn believes bad news should be delivered swiftly and she often delays good news for the right moment because she wants to share the moment. We listened to a wonderful e-book on a trip to the mountains one weekend. It was *Eat That Frog* by Brian Tracy. He said that if you face the toughest communication first, eat that frog, then the rest of your day is a piece of cake. We try to eat our frogs but some days seem to be a steady diet of the slimy things. In the end, it is good advice. Face the tough communications. Your clients deserve it. This is the super in super communicator.

My rules are shorter. Actually it's a definition: Communication is not the sending or leaving of the message. It is the confirmation of the receipt of the message. Until you know they heard and understood you, you haven't communicated. How is that possible in this busy world? After all, if you leave a voicemail or send a text, that should be the end of it. Shouldn't the other party bear some responsibility for opening their voicemail or looking at their phone? No, if you are to be a communicator, it is on you.

There is a simple solution that works 95 percent of the time and the other 5 percent you simply say it or send it again. Just end all your messages with a question. If they don't respond with an answer then you can figure they don't have it yet. An example of this is when you are speaking to a person or an audience, you occasionally ask if they agree or not to make sure they haven't drifted off. Salespeople call this qualifying as they seek agreement to their pitch at each point along the way. And this is face to face. You can imagine when the communication is written, recorded, or digital. Get confirmation that you are being heard to be sure you are communicating.

So, there it is. It really is that simple and yet so many ignore this jewel. Be a sharer of information and you too can be a super agent.

The Third Super Power

A friend I know was complaining the other day. It seems he just got back from a conference, for which he had shelled out big bucks, only to have life slap him in the face the first hour back in the office. He had gotten stoked over the three days out of town and now wondered why he even bothered. This is the motivation elevator and it is packed with fellow passengers going forever up and down.

Another friend I know who is an agent was saying he didn't know what to do. He had shown these clients more than a hundred homes and they still had not pulled the trigger and bought. He lamented that there was nothing left on the market that fit their criteria and he was reduced to checking for new listings each morning in hopes of finding these clients another home to look at.

The power to motivate yourself and others is the third super power and for many the inability to do so looms like an ogre blocking your chance at success. This should not be the case because your solution is so easy you will laugh at your past reticence when you come to understand what motivation is and how easy it is to manifest in every corner of your life.

JoAnn doesn't like that in Arizona our real estate licenses say *Salesperson*. She will explain that there is no way you can make a client buy a house they don't want and, therefore, we should not be called salespeople. But let me tell you, JoAnn is the greatest salesperson I've ever known because she sells everybody in every conversation all the time. Robert Kiyosaki of *Rich Dad Poor Dad* fame says that every investor is first a good businessperson and that every businessperson is a good salesperson. The trouble is "salesperson" is scary to many people. It was to me. I was terribly shy in high school and my uncle told me I should learn sales to overcome my introversion. That concept kept me down for years.

Let's call sales for what it is and say it is the ability to motivate somebody. It is less ominous that way. People talk about a born salesperson and I am intimidated because I was born anything but. But nobody talks about a born motivator so we will stick with that.

How do you get off that motivation elevator? How do you push the penthouse button once, and permanently enjoy the view from the top? Understand that motivation comes from you or it comes from others. If it comes from you, then you must you must be the engine of your desires and if you run out of gas, it is up to you to refill the tank. Some people can do this. They can self-talk in the mirror, eliminate negative people in their surroundings, read books, go to seminars, or they can find an easier way. The answer, at least in real estate, is to let your motivation come from your clients. At Those Callaways, we define care as taking on our clients' hopes and dreams and ambitions and making them our own. We talk about becoming the client. We become our clients' champion sent to do battle for them. Clients are a bottomless source of desires and if we make what we do about them instead of about ourselves, we will never be without motivation again.

That's great, you say, but what about motivating others? If your motivation comes from them, then how does that work? First of all, I didn't say your motivation comes from others. I said it comes from your clients. Your motivation comes from those you serve. For the rest of the population, your ability to motivate will rely on your understanding of what they want and finding ways to make them want what you have.

Let's take the agent who has shown these nice people a hundred homes. If it does not end well (and it probably won't) and you ask the prospective purchasers what went wrong, they will say something about how their agent didn't know what they wanted and kept showing them the wrong houses. It never occurs to them that what they wanted did not exist and for that poor agent it never occurred to question what these clients wanted and to help them adjust to the realities of what was available. What a terrible waste.

How do you find out what they want? How do you avoid the tragedy above? You ask and you listen. If you do not ask you won't learn and if you do not listen you won't know what to ask next. All sales, all motivation, is simply a process of asking the right questions until you get to the one that closes the deal.

That's it. Get your motivation from your clients, ask questions and listen to the answers. You will be a super motivator in no time. You can do that.

The Fourth Super Power

All right, you are putting your clients first, you are communicating, you are motivating yourself and others, you are over halfway there. Now you have to go on defense. The first three super powers are proactive, they are all about advancing and going forth but the fourth super power is all about not going backward. I'm not talking about taking a break or simply not pushing forward. I'm talking about the things that tempt and destroy because the fourth super power is professionalism. Ours is a profession and we should never forget that. We have responsibilities. We have ethical standards. We have rules to live by and many an agent has fallen victim to ignoring those rules and standards. They forget their responsibilities and lose themselves to self-interest. They give us all a bad name and our only solution is to be a shining example for others and ourselves.

You can take pride in our profession because we are the backbone of our country. We are the reason this country is a bastion of home ownership. The American dream is only possible because we help make it a reality.

Real estate agents have an opportunity to help people. It is a wonderful profession populated with good hearts. JoAnn rarely misses a chance to tell audiences that if you want to find a good citizen, find a real estate agent. Agents care about their neighborhood, their schools, crime rates, and fire protection. They participate in local government and contribute to charitable causes. Every day, agents help people through what is often their largest financial transaction, filled with emotion, doubt, and stress. The rewards, as measured in satisfaction, are enormous.

How do we practice professionalism? We take pride in what we do and we protect it in our every action. We take our paperwork seriously. We protect our client, our broker and all the other parties to the transaction. We believe in fairness. We believe in disclosure. We believe in our laws and we abide by them.

A super agent is a super professional.

The Fifth Super Power

Our final super power completes our defense. It protects what we earn and saves us from financial ruin. The fifth super power is super accountability.

You must treat your practice as a business or it will forever remain a hobby, an avocation, a way to make a little money that stops the moment you stop working. You might as well work for wages.

This is where so many agents fail. They are good agents, they are super professionals but they are subject to the vagaries of the market, they run afoul of the IRS, they throw away money in the form of unrecognized assets, they live above their means, they go broke, they start over and over again. Agents who don't appreciate what a privilege it is to be an agent, switch twice a year from brokers who would do anything to help them succeed to a new broker because they are looking for the right deal, not realizing that the right deal is the one they make for themselves. They refuse to treat their practice as a business and as a consequence, it never becomes the wonderful asset and vehicle to financial security that it can be.

The pity is that it is so easy. Today, you do not have to be an accountant, you just need to keep good records and that is made easy with cheap software. What you need more than anything is a healthy respect for your numbers. You need to decide what metrics you should track and then track them relentlessly.

Secondly, you must realize that a business is not a bucket of money you keep emptying. A business is a financial system into which you make an investment in hopes of making a profit after expenses. So many agents believe they can practice this profession without investing so much as a dime out of their pockets. They pay their broker fees, which they resent. They are late with their association dues because they think they are too high. And they are the last to pitch in at closing with any small unexpected expense that the paying of would forever endear their client to them and by refusing a little help they lose that client forever.

Finally, you cannot spend all you make in excessive advertising and promotion and call yourself profitable. We know agents who are so competitive, so desirous of the spotlight, that they sell millions of dollars of real estate and have nothing to show for it. The shame is that they only realize their folly when the money is gone because they were not keeping track with a $100 to $200 package of software.

These are the five super powers:

1. The power to put your clients first.
2. The power to communicate.
3. The power to motivate.
4. The power to be professional.
5. The power to be accountable and treat your practice as a business.

What is amazing about these is that they are yours for the asking. You don't need a fancy car, or a fashion-star wardrobe. You don't even need a powerful computer. You can be a super agent with no more than a smartphone and Internet access.

Chapter 2 Summary

The First Super Power Is the Power to Put Your Client First

- The three keys are: Honesty, Competence, and Care.
- You must hold all three keys whole and complete, partial keys do not count.
- Make the commitment, speak the commitment, and keep the commitment.

The Second Super Power Is the Power to Communicate

- Understand the basic human need for information.
- Never forget that clients don't understand the complexities.
- JoAnn's rules: Return all calls before you can go home and do the tough ones first.
- Joseph's definition: Communication is confirmation of the receipt of the information.

The Third Super Power Is the Power to Motivate

- Sales is the ability to motivate.
- Motivate yourself by focusing on your client's motivations.
- Motivate others by asking questions and listening for the answer.
  (The first three super powers are your offense and the last two are your defense.)

The Fourth Super Power Is the Power of Professionalism

- Be proud of your profession.
- Follow the rules.
- Protect all parties.

The Fifth Super Power Is the Power of Accountability

- Treat your practice as a business.
- Be willing to invest in your business.
- Guard against overspending.

3

Starting Out Fast

Whether you are newly licensed or restarting your career, the opportunities are boundless. This is one of the most exciting times of your life. You get to start with a blank page. You get to be the architect of your future, the inventor of Agent You. But wait, you say. A blank page can be intimidating. You don't know what you want to be or do. You are afraid. That's okay. That's normal. Let's put all that aside for a moment. We will get to the confusion and fear part and erase it like a wet rag on a chalkboard. For now though, let's rejoice. You are starting out, it's a wonderful time, and you are starting out fast.

That's how I look back on us. It was an incredible time and we were incredibly lucky. JoAnn and I almost stumbled into success. We didn't really deserve it. We hadn't worked long and hard in preparation for success. Maybe you could say life had prepared us. We were where a lot of people find themselves, halfway through life and no further along than the day we graduated high school. It didn't seem like a blessing at the time but we needed the money and that outweighed the fear. We were willing to try anything.

We picked our broker based on proximity to our house. John Hall and Associates was the closest real estate office to where we lived. We chose our area of specialization by walking out our front door and putting 50 business cards in our neighbor's doorjambs. I didn't knock or anything. I didn't want to talk to anyone. I didn't know what to say. Later we learned that this was the last place to start. We lived in an area of old houses on acre lots, too far apart with long-time residents who seldom moved. All the action, we were told, was in North Scottsdale with new construction and transient executives moving every two years. We made every mistake and yet success found us.

Choices

Were we to have the opportunity to do it all over again I might make some changes but, for all our awkwardness, we did many things right; so here is my advice on some basic choices you need to make.

Choose a broker near where you live. I'm not saying there is no difference in brokers, far from it. Every broker is unique and sincere in what they offer but in the end your success will come from you. Your broker will be your resource, your mentor, your confidant, your cheerleader. He or she will want you to do well, but they will not do it for you. So you may as well spend less time commuting and more time with clients.

Don't chase the money. Don't go to the hot new area. First of all the competition will be fierce and second of all the money is everywhere. In our sleepy little square mile where we began, there are a thousand homes. Over the last decade and a half we have sold half of them and some houses we have sold several times. The money, wherever you are, is right under your feet.

Sell what you know and understand. I'm not saying you can't learn newer homes if you live in an older one or you can't sell HUD repos while living in a McMansion but when you can relate to the property and the owner it is easier, and when you are starting out fast, easy is better.

Feel free to choose a specialty or not to choose one. Many times JoAnn and I have been asked, "What is your specialty?" And we respond that our specialty is relationships, which is code for we don't have one. Remember, we needed the money, so we took on anything and everything. We also had no preference or hobbies, unless you want to count our love for books, in which case we could specialize in the sale of libraries. But we know many agents who find a niche and the combination of work and play can be fulfilling. Our daughter is a quilter and regularly brings clients who share her passion. I know agents who specialize in golf properties, horse properties, cheap condos, luxury condos, rentals, investment homes, and the list goes on. I also know many agents just like us, with nothing more than an adventurous spirit. Whatever you choose, just be sure you do it out of passion; as Confucius said, "if you love what you do, you will never work another day in your life."

Whatever you choose, get educated. Know that taking the required hours of classes and passing the state test are only the beginning. You must become competent in all you do. Take all the training your broker offers. Take all the classes your association offers.

Look into designations, not for the letters you can put after your name, but for the wealth of knowledge these programs offer. Ours is a supportive industry and you should take advantage of every educational opportunity you can.

Associate yourself with winners, not losers. Jim Rohn, mentor to the likes of Tony Robbins and Jack Canfield, once said, "You are the average of the five people you spend the most time with." Spend your time wisely. Go to events. Listen to panels. Identify who is like the person you want to be and introduce yourself. Follow the stars and you will gain your own light in the sky.

Coaches and mentors are available. Most are very capable and can take you to the next level but one caution here—learn the basics first. I'm sure an Olympic skating coach can take a five-year-old and teach them to skate but that coach's value would be unrealized in the beginning. The child needs to get their balance first and spend time on the ice before they start learning the art of a sit spin or how to do a double axel.

Basic Requirements

Speaking of basics lets go through the list of initial needs. You must have business cards, if for no other reason than to give to older clients who expect them. Actually, used correctly, they can be a novelty to younger generations and set you apart from agents who only have e-cards or transfer their information from one digital device to the next like a fist bump. Yes, you must also have all your information digitally available for texting, e-mailing, or messaging through a social media channel or on an app. Clients, other agents, lenders, title companies, and so on must know who you are and how to reach you. Prepare this contact info with pride. Create an e-mail signature.

Own the smartest phone you can. I heard an agent the other day describe a smaller urban area as backward. She said agents there don't want e-mail on their phones because it might ruin their day. She was kidding but I know plenty of agents who resist change and abhor technology. Don't be one of them. Embrace the advances that come along every day, just don't think they are replacing you.

You are an agent now. You are special. Everything you say and do should support that fact. Wear appropriate attire, have appropriate transportation. Does this mean you have to wear a suit and tie or drive a luxury sedan? Of course not. JoAnn and I wear pressed jeans and drive a Buick but we shampoo and shower every morning. I don't go out without shaving. Our nails are trimmed and clean and the car goes through the car wash at least once a week, more if it rains. When we open our mouths the words are polite and courteous. If you can do that, you are an agent.

Your One Purpose

What to do first? What to do next? We are back to that blank page and this is where many new agents fail without even having a chance to begin. They just do not know what to do next. They suffer from too many choices or choosing between difficult things and they become frozen.

We promised you easy and here it is. You only have one purpose, one thing to do—make a deal. For all the technology, training, education, networking, and previewing inventory, for all that, you really have only one mission and that is to make a deal, and in making that deal you will have created a client, and that client will make you rich. You see this is not as a business of many transactions; it is a game of one transaction completed well and then repeated many times.

Let me tell you about our first deal. We had been bumbling along and had gotten a listing in our neighborhood, the result of those business cards stuck in doorjambs. JoAnn and I were holding open houses and meeting potential buyers and were carting them around in our leased Park Avenue with no immediate success. Then, as we passed a for-sale-by-owner (FSBO - pronounced Fisbo) sign a few blocks from our listing, one of these buyers asked, "how much is that one?" We said we didn't know but later we went back without the prospect in our car. I got out and snuck up to the flyer box on the post, grabbed a copy, and jumped back in the car. As we fled the scene, I told JoAnn that it was the last flyer in the holder. Well, I might as well have admitted to starving a child so JoAnn said we had go get more flyers. We went to a print shop and had 20 copies made with what seemed like my last $5.

We returned to the scene and as I snuck up on the post the owner stepped out her front door and asked just what was I doing. I fumbled through an explanation and she seemed satisfied. Then she told me her husband was handy and that if I knew of any fix-ups in the area to let her know. Silly me, I thought she was singling me out for the flyer kindness. I now know that as a FSBO, agents regularly visited her and she told them all the same thing. But I didn't know any better and the next day we got up the courage to call and tell her about a house we had seen during our fruitless travels with other prospects who did not see the potential.

She said they would meet us at the house and we met her husband an hour later. He gave it the once-over and said he would call his bank. He had a cell phone the size of a brick, but this was 1997 and we were impressed. He dialed and said, "Hi, Mom?" We later met this lovely lady, long after we already knew she loved her son and whatever he said was just great with her. We wrote a cash offer and had our first commission check five days later.

I tell you this not because it was easy. Remember, we had been working hard for a couple of months. We taxied a lot of lookers. We held a bunch of open houses. We had experienced many embarrassments. We deserved a break and it came along, but what you need to know is this. Last year this couple's two little girls suddenly grew up and both got married. When our grandson took them out and found each a home, our database counted them as sale numbers 101 and 102 stemming from that original first sale.

Over the years we sold the sister's house and found her and her husband another one. Then they got divorced and had to each have a new house. Then he got remarried and his new bride wanted a home of her own instead of his bachelor pad. Then when they divorced his new ex used us to find her a new home—and the list goes on and on.

What to Do Now

All you need to do is make that one deal. Then you make the next deal. Then you make the next one, and each time they come a little closer together and each time you learn what works and what doesn't work for you. That's right, you are unique, you are special, you are not a cookie-cutter agent and what works for you may not work for anybody else and conversely what works for another may not work for you.

The answer to what you should do now and what you should do next must come from you and you must come to know the answer. You must get up in the morning and know what you are doing. Not knowing is a terrible thing. Let's talk about some things that apply to everybody so you may find your unique way.

Scripts

You must develop your own scripts and the only way you create an answer for every question is by talking to people. Ultimately, you must be comfortable talking to people about what you do and how you do it. You must put yourself in front of people and talk,

talk, talk. You will embarrass yourself. We did. I say stupid stuff every day. But talk you must. In time you will know what to say and when to say it. You will have your own scripts.

Another word about talking, you must also listen. A super agent is a super motivator and that comes from asking questions and listening to the answers. Later, after you've talked to someone, work out all the things you should have said. This is where the real work is done. The more you say to yourself next time I will say this, the closer you are to saying it better.

Circle of Influence

Okay, you now have your one purpose, make a deal, and you know your first step is to become comfortable talking about real estate. How do you put these together? How do you make the talking part lead to a deal and how do you make it easy? The first question every broker asks every new agent is if they have contacted their circle of influence. Some brokers leave it at that and some go into the idea in great detail, but here are some fresh thoughts you may not have heard.

First of all: it is not about the circle, it is all about the influence. Your circle of influence is everyone you know and especially everyone who knows you. You should sit down and make a list and make it as long as you can. Think of every relative, friend, high school classmate, fellow members at church, or any other organization to which you belong, former coworkers, where you spend your money, your doctor, your dentist, everybody you can possibly come up with. This is your circle and you want to stretch it as big as you can. Input these into a spreadsheet or Outlook or a CRM (customer relations manager) software program and then notify your circle that you are now in real estate. Not much will come of this initial contact but if you continue to contact them with an update or newsletter you will eventually get business from this database. This is your circle.

Now look at your circle and decide with whom you have the most influence and who has the most influence with you. This is your primary target. This is who you should be talking real estate with. You may only have a few people on this list, two to five, or you may have more. The idea is to grow this inner circle through personal contact. I already know your next question, so let me offer you a simple way to introduce the subject. Create a short list of questions and ask for help. Make a time, treat it as an appointment, and explain it as a training exercise or assignment necessary to your getting started in real estate. Present it as a survey you must complete in person.

You may have more but here are the questions you must include.

1. How many times have you bought or sold a home?
2. Did you use an agent?
3. Was it a good experience and why?
4. Did you have a bad experience and why?
5. Who do you know that is thinking of buying or selling real estate in the next month?

Prepare and present this in whatever form is most comfortable for you but here is an idea. Print your questions in a large font on a single sheet of paper and insert it into a plastic page protector. Simply hand your survey to your friend and record their answers on a pad or iPad. Be sure to identify each set of answers with a name and date as this will go into your new database. This may seem incredibly simple, and it is, but each time you complete an interview you will learn and become more comfortable with talking real estate. As you do this you will become comfortable with expanding your inner circle of influence. In time you will drop the survey and find yourself asking perfect strangers, and the best part of all is that these interviews will lead you to that first deal and then the next and the next.

Open House for Beginners

What if you have no circle of influence? We didn't. Check that, we had a circle but we were too shy to do anything with it. Looking back we really were lame. Anyway, we had no circle so we had to find another way to talk to people. Chapter 12 is devoted to open houses, but here we need to discuss open house for beginners, open house as strictly a learning tool, a way to talk to people.

Our first open house wasn't even our listing. It belonged to another agent in our office who identified our true talents—we were free help. She showed us the ropes and looking back, most of what she showed us was wrong but she had this one listing. It was vacant and backed to a busy street and she wasn't going to sit it open so she offered the opportunity to us. We went the day before and washed the windows and cleaned the floors. We bought signs and showed up early. We immediately turned on the lights, and opened the rear slider. The traffic roar poured in so we just spoke a little louder. The home was in a good neighborhood and we got good traffic from curious lookers wanting to know about the area. We stumbled along and embarrassed ourselves. We held this home open three weekends in a row and each time we had better answers. We didn't sell the home but we were better agents for the experience.

You might do better than JoAnn and me. It won't be hard. You might even sell the house you're sitting. You might pick up a client and show them other homes and then sell one of those. The beauty of open house is that at any given moment you might just make a deal and remember, your single focus is to make a deal.

Bear in mind, you're new and your talent is that you have the time that other agents don't. Make yourself available and get permission to open another agent's open house. This is your opportunity to talk to people and talking to people is your avenue to that first deal.

This is how you start out fast. Make that first deal and then put that client first. Become a super communicator. Learn to talk about real estate, to ask questions, and listen to the answers. Take on the super powers one at a time and the first one you want is to be a super motivator.

Chapter 3 Summary

Choices

- Your broker.
- Your area.
- Your specialty.

Basic Requirements

- Your contact information.
- Smartphone and other technology.
- Appropriate attire, appropriate transportation, grooming, hygiene.

Your One Purpose

- Make a deal.
- Our first deal.
- 102 deals.

What to Do Now

- The answer must come from you.
- Not knowing is a terrible thing.
- Find your unique way.

Scripts

- Talking to people.
- Listen.
- Work out what you should have said.

Circle of Influence

- It's not about the circle; it's all about the influence.
- Send announcements and start a database.
- Survey your inner circle.

Open House for Beginners

- Our first open house.
- Your talent is time.
- Get permission.

4 Keep Your Golden Ticket

First, be a good agent.

Every day the rules get broken and bad things happen. I had an instructor at a continuing education class begin his session by posing a question. He asked, "What is the one way to practice safe real estate?" After a short barrage of unacceptable answers he said, "No. The only way to practice safe real estate is abstinence."

After the class, JoAnn turned in her car seat to face me and said, "He's right, you know." She was really quite alarmed. I told her not to worry because I always tell JoAnn not to worry but it hung in the air all the way home. In the end we agreed that renewal classes were something you had to take followed by a period of withdrawal symptoms. We would have to recommit to being good agents and do a lot of knocking on wood.

Over the years we've come up with five magic rules to a spotless record. We know real estate is not practiced the same in every state and you have to learn what applies in your jurisdiction but these rules are universal and unchanging. They have become ingrained in our team and us and they have served us well. Read them carefully. Return to them after an alarming class or seminar. While there is no way to predict what may come out of the woodwork, these will keep you 99 percent safe. They will allow you to first be a good agent.

Our first managing broker was Marge Lindsay and we saw her often. Sometimes we called her but more often she called us. Were it not for her tutelage and guidance we would not be licensed today. These first three rules came from Marge and we want to give her credit and special mention here.

Rule One—It's All in the Contract

The contract is everything. It should cover every agreement between the parties and it should be clear as to each party's intention. Ambiguity has no place in this legal document. Your buyer or seller must understand what they are signing and you must be prepared to explain the nuances of every word to your client.

In Arizona, our contracts and forms are created by our state association and the purchase contract gets updated every couple of years because our industry's standard of care finds new protections to be included for either the buyer or the seller. The document is designed not to favor one party over the other but to protect each. We respect the doctrine of fair treatment to all parties and we do not strike out the boilerplate or printed language. If our client has changes, additional terms, or deletions, we write them in so the other party sees our client's intent clearly.

In your career you will encounter clients and agents who wish to wander from this path of conformity. Do not be deluded or tricked. If something smells fishy, then you may as well get out the pepper and lemon. Here are just a few red flags to listen for:

- "We will address that later." Contracts never improve after the signatures are affixed. Of course, you may find your client needs to renegotiate as situations evolve: timelines need extending, repairs need doing, and so on, but make every effort to fully address everything up front.
- "We'll just bump the commission up to 10 or 15 percent." Agents are free to set commissions but if the average in your area is around three percent, and the other agent is suggesting three or four times that, someone is being defrauded and you want nothing to do with it.
- "We'll handle that outside escrow." No, no, no. Everything, every dollar, must be on the HUD-1 or closing sheet. Now an argument can be made for a separate bill of sale on some patio furniture the buyer just fell in love with at the home inspection but don't let that lull you into justifying a seller renting back on a separate lease after a short sale.
- "We won't tell the bank that or we will give the bank a different version." It is fine for your client to not want the other party to know their true intent when negotiating, but the contract should be an instrument of full disclosure, to all parties, for all material issues which would affect a party's decision to buy or sell.

Keep an ear open for these no-no's and say no. Remember, when in doubt, don't do it. Bear in mind that Marge gave us this rule because we were breaking it. We spent so much time fixing things in the beginning. I would ask Marge for some sort of handbook and she would patiently reply, "It's all in the contract." I would go away and spit wooden nickels until I had read and reread the offending clause. Ultimately, I had to figure out what each line meant and I had to be able to explain the consequences of each action a client might take. Eventually I realized that Marge started every conversation with, "Well, what does the contract say?" and, eventually, I stopped seeing Marge and today I say these same words when something comes up. Learn your contract.

Rule Two—Be the Source of the Source

There is a temptation in this business to want to know everything and to want to help your client by volunteering advice. Now part of your unique value proposition is your knowledge of the market and your experience in real estate matters. But do not confuse that with being the source of every little jewel of information.

Years ago, as a young man, I found myself in the Army's basic training. It was day two and we had all fallen out in the company street, which means we were standing in five rows of 10, groups of 50, and there were about 300 of us. We faced the First Sergeant's office, which was on the second floor of the center barracks building and he came out on his balcony to address us. He asked in a booming voice if any among us had a chauffeur's license, and a young man from the south, by way of his accent, raised his hand and said, "I do."

The First Sergeant told him to get on up here and I can still remember vividly the sound of the recruit's new boots on the wooden stairs for it was deathly quiet. Upon his arrival the First Sergeant said in a loud voice for all to hear, "Well, let me see it," and the poor fellow dug it out of his old wallet from his new fatigues pants. The First Sergeant examined it carefully and said, "This is expired."

"Oh no," the volunteer said as he pointed to the card, "I just renewed it last month."

The First Sergeant nodded gravely and in that resounding voice every man in that street will never forget, said, "You go into my office and chauffeur that buffer over my floors until I can see my reflection without so much as bending over."

I got it. We all got it. The Army doesn't want volunteers acting in their own initiative—they want obedience. Oh, there was plenty of volunteering in the Army but it always came from someone of higher rank in the form of an order.

Your client doesn't want your opinion unless they ask for it. When they do ask for information, they will hold you or the source responsible. Always be the source of the source. If they want to know about schools, give them a report from the school district. If they want to know about crime, direct them to a website.

If they want to know about that smell, arrange an inspection. I don't care if your previous career was as a general contractor—don't be their inspector. Don't measure the house, have an appraiser do it. Don't price the house, show them the comps. Be the source of the source and you will never run a buffer over the First Sergeant's floor again.

Rule Three—It Is Always Up to the Client

This one gets broken so often, every day, that I must explain by example.

We have a nice agent in town who thinks everything is up to him. We call him with a contract and he says no, it is not enough money. We then ask if he has presented the offer to his client and he says not yet.

We were negotiating repairs last week with a nice lady. It was day three on a five-day timeline and when we bogged down on a roof repair, she said, as if it was an imposition, "I guess I'll just have to call my client then."

Every day we deal with agents who speak for and decide for their clients and it is a tragedy. In some twisted way they must think they are protecting the client, or controlling the situation, or some other justification. In fact, they are misleading their clients and the day of reckoning is soon at hand.

Your clients do not need controlling—they need service. Your clients do not need protecting through misinformation or information withheld. They need protection that only the truth and full disclosure can provide. This is where the rubber meets the road. If you are to be a super agent with super powers, you must put your clients first. You must be honest and competent and care enough not to treat your clients like children but as the adults they are, fully capable of making their own decisions. It is theirs to make, always.

Rule Four—Obedience Must Be Legal

Every agent gets this mixed up sooner or later. What we are talking about here is your fiduciary responsibility, the definition of which is abused daily. I've had agents mix up fiduciary with being fair to all parties or as a justification to not be fair. Not true. Other agents say it is being financially accountable to their client. This is partly true. Still others go into an explanation of their client's best interest but then they don't know what those interests are. Part of the confusion is that the definition of fiduciary in real estate representation varies from book to book and teacher to teacher. My definition of fiduciary is obedience. It is all up to the client and we must do as we are instructed.

We learned this the hard way (as if there were any other way?) on a simple transaction that went wildly wrong. We had a listing and a buyer wanted to make an offer. There was no other agent, which made us dual agents representing both buyer and seller. We wrote the contract and were told the earnest-money check would be good as soon as the buyer got back to St. Louis and transferred funds. We presented the offer and told the sellers that the check was not yet good. They countered, we faxed back and forth to our buyer, and made a deal. We asked about the check and were told to hold it another few days. We told our seller and opened escrow with a dollar from our own pocket. If you've been an agent awhile you already know where this is going. To make a long story short, the first check bounced and a replacement check bounced, and then the deal fell apart under circumstances that made the seller feel the earnest money should be forfeited, but there was no earnest money because we thought we were being obedient to our buyer and we had kept the seller informed. We ended up covering the earnest money ourselves and our broker explained it to me. Fiduciary means obedience, but the order must be legal. When a client asks or instructs you to do something that is in conflict with the law, your commissioner's rules, your association's code of ethics, or any other standard by which you may judge it wrong, you must say no and find another way for your client to succeed legally. Remember, obedience must be legal and you will sail in safe harbors.

Rule Five—Disclose Early, Disclose Often

A material fact is any information that might affect a buyers decision to purchase and/or how much to pay. The same goes for the seller except a material fact affects their decision to sell and/or at what price. Think about that. How can you possibly predict what matters to a buyer or seller ahead of time? But in the clear light of 20/20 hindsight the most mundane detail can loom large and cause regret and suspicion. You and your client have an obligation to disclose all material facts.

This does not extend to how much more your buyer is willing to pay or the real motivation for your seller to sell. You have an obligation to protect your client's best interest and to be obedient as long as their instructions are legal. This is where so many agents get stuck in a moral dilemma. If your buyer tells you not to disclose something that you know should be disclosed, you must sell that client on disclosure being in their best interest. The only way to protect you and your client is to err on the side of disclosure, rather than attempting to walk the line of just-enough disclosure.

By far, the majority of post-closing claims stem from failure to disclose. Your state, no doubt has abundant case law on the subject that you can and should delve into as much possible. For our purposes here, you should advise your clients to disclose early and disclose often.

In the practical world, there is a lot of nondisclosure that, while not leading to litigation, leads to ill will and can affect your success. We had a seller in the Biltmore area, one of our more expensive neighborhoods, who was wonderfully cooperative and very pleased with the job we were doing. The buyer's agent was one of the best in town. We were all one big happy transaction. Then we had the pre-closing walk-through.

While standing in the backyard with both agents and both clients, the buyer stepped on something hard and metallic. Upon examination, which involved everyone squatting or getting down on hands and knees, we discovered the end of a buried pipe that the seller said led to an abandoned propane tank. You would have thought we had just defamed the buyer's children and the war began. The seller said he thought it too unimportant to mention. He had poured the 500-gallon tank full of sand years before and cut the pipe flush with the ground. The buyer found the explanation questionable and the wife feared we were all standing on an unexploded bomb.

In the end, we were able to get it all fixed but the bad taste ruined it for everybody. Since that day we ask our seller early and we ask our buyer often. We tell our clients that the truth is the one thing that will protect them. Disclose, disclose, disclose.

I know an agent who routinely saves up her disclosures for just before closing. She explains the delay with her desire to be sure before reducing things to paper. Every time she does this, I want to tell her this only causes suspicion. As her last-minute disclosures come piling in, the other party always wonders what else have they not been told. Disclose early.

It is often not practical to know everything that needs to be disclosed. These things come up during the escrow period and as they do, you must race to disclose them as soon as possible. Your diligence and speed will be recognized and appreciated. Disclose often.

Finally, there is the agent who fears losing the deal. They hold back and take a wait-and-see attitude, as if closing will make the issue go away. Believe me, you don't want those deals. They will grey your hair and interrupt your sleep. And when one comes back to haunt you, the commission is nothing compared to the consequences. Disclose early and disclose often.

Respect What You Do

These five rules will protect and guide you in the practice of real estate. If you give them the respect they deserve, they will keep you out of trouble.

When JoAnn and I were young and foolish, I got a job in a steel-fabrication plant. The hourly rate was triple what I had earned up to that point and I was so proud the day I got my Boilermaker's Union Card. But during my first day on the job a guy almost got killed loading a rail car because he failed to double-check a come-along jack that came unlocked. It happened during my second hour. I had on my new steel-toed boots, my heavy leather gloves, my safety glasses and my shiny, unscathed hard hat and I watched them pull in the ambulance and haul that family man away on a gurney. My trainer, a journeyman welder, explained it to me: "Everything here is heavier than it looks. It can cut off your finger or crush your leg or crack your skull the first time you put your hard hat anywhere other than on your head."

I remember being afraid, truly afraid for weeks. I felt I was in a steel jungle being stalked by some future tragedy. Had we not needed the money I would have quit the first day, but I lasted the better part of a year before getting promoted to the office where I could watch those brave men clock in and out each day. Looking back, I became very casual about the plant. The jungle effect faded and I worked hard and appreciated the opportunity. But I always took it seriously. Every time I put on my hard hat I remembered my mentor's warning and I respected what we all did.

Not much has changed. Real estate is not a steel plant but it has its own dangers and you should take them seriously and respect what you do. But that danger should not stand in the way of your success. Although small by today's standards those wages looked bigger back then than the money we make today. That higher income elevated our family and gave us a higher standard of living. I didn't quit that first day and neither should you.

Your broker is your best friend. Your broker will look out for you and help you and stand up for you and keep you out of trouble. Your broker is your hard hat and you should never let it leave your head.

As a friend you must return the favor by protecting your broker. Always think risk reduction. Be a good agent. Remember, it is all in the contract, be the source of the source, it is always the client's decision, obedience must be legal, and disclose early, disclose often.

A super agent is a super rule follower, not out of fear, but out of respect. Respect your clients. Respect your fellow agents. Respect your broker and respect your opportunity. This is the greatest profession in the world and you should not let anyone take it away from you, especially yourself.

Always put your clients first, communicate, motivate, be professional and accountable. Do the right thing and keep that golden ticket.

Chapter 4 Summary

First, be a good agent.

There Are Five Rules to Keep Your Record Spotless

- It's all in the contract.
- Be the source of the source.
- It is always the client's decision.
- Obedience must be legal.
- Disclose early, disclose often.

Respect What You Do

- Take it seriously.
- Don't let fear take away your opportunity.
- Protect your broker and think risk reduction.

5 Everything You Need to Know about Working with Buyers

We talk about buyers and sellers as if they were two separate species, but the truth is every transaction has one of each. Buyers are often selling their prior home and sellers are often buying their next one. When we differentiate between buyers and sellers we are really talking about two distinct and opposite sets of emotions existing within one host.

A buyer, therefore, is a client or prospective client who is currently experiencing buyer emotions. They have only one goal and that is to obtain the object of their desire. They covet, want, and become self-absorbed in their quest for accomplishing their goal. Because they are the source of the funds, they feel a sense of importance. Without their demand, supply would have no value and yet, they suffer a sense of futility and a fear of failure. Because they do not purchase a home often, the process can be intimidating; but with the advances of technology, buyer clients are experiencing a new emotion—empowerment.

The Empowered Client

Home ownership boomed in the United States after World War II as the GI Bill and the baby boom gave birth to the suburbs and the American dream became a reality for millions. With this explosion came the empowered real estate agent and the Multiple Listing Service. Up to that time agents would represent a list of properties and buyers would have to go from agent to agent to look at what that agent had. The MLS, as the Multiple Listing

Service came to be called, was created as a way for agents to share their listings and commissions with other agents in hopes of expanding exposure, as other agents brought buyers to their listings and vice versa. For the next 50 years, this arrangement put the agent at the center of the real estate transaction. The agent had all the information and a buyer needed an agent to get access to it. This has all changed.

Today, a buyer can access everything there is to know about homes for sale in any area at any time. They can sit in their kitchen at 2 a.m. with their digital device and search to their heart's content. If they wish, they can compare prices, look at recent sales, and learn as much as any agent about the process of purchasing their next home. Some buyers do all these things and, as technology improves, more buyers will. The client is constantly becoming more and more empowered.

Many agents have struggled with this change. Their model has always been the dependent client and they have built their business around currying that dependence. This approach still works. After all, not all clients care to be empowered but their numbers are declining, and those agents who won't or don't change will find themselves with fewer and fewer clients.

The super agent, on the other hand, embraces this change and embraces the empowered client. In fact, the more empowered the better. But this change has altered the dynamic of working with buyers. We have moved from directing the client to serving them and this is where the super power of putting the client first makes all the difference. As a super agent, you must put the client at the center of the transaction. You must give up control. Your value proposition must change from proprietary information to the glue of super service. This works just as well for those clients who don't wish to be empowered. Your service must include information and the interpretation of that information, but you must also be completely honest, totally competent, and provide unwavering care. This is the power through which you will attract and keep clients experiencing the emotional turmoil of buying a home.

Russell Shaw, a fellow super agent and good friend, explains buyers this way. "Buyers are looking for a house, not an agent. Nobody ever got on the computer and said, 'I hope I find a good agent today.' Buyers are struggling with many emotions, but loyalty to an agent is not one of them."

So why would you want to work with buyers? Quite simply, they have the money and if you can understand their emotions, a portion of that money can be yours very quickly. Just remember, this is a service business and you must serve these buyers by putting them first.

The Three Cares about Your Buyer

There are three things you must know about your buyer. You must know their:

1. Motivation: What are their goals and dreams?
2. Capacity: What can they afford?
3. Expectations: What is their criteria?

We call these *the three cares* about your buyer because if you don't care about these, you will have no idea how to serve your buyer. Your buyer will know you don't know and don't care and will feel no loyalty to you. You will have no glue.

This may seem obvious, but agents fail to care about these three things every day. A buyer says they want to see this house or that house and the agent hops in the car without so much as asking why. They show homes in whatever price range the buyer sets without asking the client to get with a lender. They ask the buyer's criteria and exhaust what's available on the MLS. Then they put the clients on a new listings e-mail feed forever. All this because they never cared enough to help the client modify their criteria to what is available. Why do agents do this? Partly it is out of a lack of care. They are so focused on commission they have no time for the buyer's goals. More often, they do all this out of fear. They are afraid of losing something they do not have. They equate their willingness to show and lack of nonprying questions with service and the buyer feels no loyalty.

A super agent presses for information. A super agent motivates with questions. The buyer finds their way and often comes to know more about themselves in the process. The super agent's questions get buyers where they want to be. Care enough to know your buyer's motivations, capacity and criteria. This is service.

Finding Property

With the advances of technology and the empowered client's help, the search for the right home has become easier in some ways and more difficult in others. Because your prospective buyer may already have a ton of information, you have to work hard at having more information and at being prepared to interpret that information. Your super competence will save you and will serve your clients. Knowing your market, what is available, and what recently sold, is your goal.

I believe Noel was our third or fourth client in our car who said to us how much he appreciated working with professionals who really knew their market. Now we really didn't have a clue but were showing Noel houses in our original square mile and that area we knew well. I had printed all the assessor maps for the 14 subdivisions and taped them together. This was a task much more easily completed on the computer today but back then I did it all by hand. The scale was one inch equals 100 feet and the thing covered our dining-room table. Then I looked up the history on each house, 984 in all, and wrote little coded information on each lot that had sold or otherwise been on the market. It was a lot of work and looked ugly with all my scratch marks. I had to fold it up like a roadmap so it could fit in a file folder. I had done all this during the month before Noel and his wife walked into our first listing on Sweetwater Avenue. So when Noel got in our car we knew our market. Thank goodness he never asked to cross 64th Street or go south of Cactus Road.

Today I can go anywhere in our valley and be knowledgeable. Between Google Earth, the county assessor records, and the MLS, I can advise on any property. This is what your buyer clients are looking for. Learn to use these tools, and be ready for when your Noel gets in your car.

The more you show the more you know but if you really want to get up to speed, preview homes on the market. Take your downtime and go look at what is available. This may well be your best time spent.

Don't ignore the FSBOs (for sale by owners) since they will probably agree to pay a commission if you bring a buyer, and knowing the price when your buyer asks can be impressive.

Ask questions. Ask the FSBOs why they are selling. When you are previewing, ask the sellers what they like and don't like about the neighborhood. Ask the neighbors when they come in to your open house. Be curious and you will become the consummate professional to that next buyer.

Finding the right property for your buyer is a matter of understanding their criteria and then combining those goals and dreams with your knowledge of the area.

Showing Property

Your broker and your association will set the standards of care in your area but you will want to keep certain things in mind. Always be courteous and punctual. When things change in the field be a super communicator. Other agents and sellers appreciate feedback. Always turn on the lights and open the window coverings, but then reverse the process to leave the home as you found it. Be sure the home is secure. Ours is a small community and what goes around comes around. Be the agent you hope other agents to be.

Once inside, it is your job to help the buyer understand the property but remember, it is their showing. They are the ones communing with the home and your contributions should be helpful, not intrusive. This is where they may live. They are placing furniture and deciding whose bedroom is whose. Ask questions but give them their space.

Sell benefits, not features. Features are the basic facts, the number of bedrooms and baths, the finishes, the cabinetry, the countertops, the square footage, the heating, the cooling, and so forth. Benefits are what those features mean to your buyer. Talk about the floor plan. Discuss how this or that fits their lifestyle. It's what they can do with those features that matter. Motivate your buyer with questions. Ask what they feel about the location, what they think about this carpet color or that brand of appliances. Answering your questions tells them more about themselves and those answers help you better serve their needs.

At the end of each showing always give your buyer an opportunity to buy. This seems so obvious but many agents dismiss this, relying instead on the buyer volunteering their interest to write an offer. Some agents are afraid to ask, again, fearing to lose something they do not have. A super agent knows to ask the most important question of all—Do you want to make an offer on this one?—because it helps the buyer to understand their own desires. To not ask this question risks the buyer thinking that they will keep this in mind as they go on looking endlessly until a super agent comes along and asks them to decide.

I was the worst salesperson in the world—shy, afraid, inexperienced—but I made this question my one rule for showing homes. At times it seemed foolish after the client had already told me they hated the house, but ask I did and they would laugh (more embarrassment), and at the end of the day I would find myself writing a contract. A contract is your goal and asking if they want to write an offer is the quickest and easiest way to get there.

Keep Showing Property

Do not give up. Once people have made a decision to buy it is like a bug they cannot shake. They will buy sooner or later. The trick is to be there when that magic moment arrives. Be honest, be competent, and care about that client and they will stick with you.

My personal record for showing homes to one client was somewhere around 100 over a period of six months. Every week or 10 days I would take the wife out to see possibilities and then, about one Sunday a month, we would have the husband along. They each had very specific criteria. She did not want to see the kitchen from the front door. He wanted a large master bath. They both wanted a three-car garage. He liked the Biltmore area. She liked Arcadia. Both of these areas were close to downtown. My clients were both lawyers for separate firms. They were blessed with a late-in-life baby and she completely absorbed their lives. They were currently more than 45 minutes away from work, so their motivation to be closer was strong.

On the last day we looked at seven out of eight homes I had pulled and they decided to settle and make an offer on number three. For some reason I broke the rule which says, "Once they agree to make an offer, write it now," and I said the number eight house was only a few blocks away and the other agent had said she would be holding it open all afternoon. So we went.

It was an older home in Arcadia that had started out as a small ranch cottage in the fifties and been expanded and remodeled several times since. The square footage was on the low side but after six months I was trying anything and the first thing we saw from the curb was a double carport. We walked in the front door and the listing agent greeted us from the highly visible kitchen. We turned left and found ourselves in a modest master bedroom separated from a modest bathroom by a glass block wall that did not reach the ceiling. They said they would take it.

The price was just shy of a million dollars and on the high side of their budget so the home had a lot to offer. It was beautiful in every detail. The yard was gorgeous, front and back. But it didn't fit their criteria. I learned that day that when buyers walk into that home meant especially for them, criteria goes out the window. Over the years, we have seen this again and again. So when you run out of homes that fit their criteria, keep showing.

Three Showings a Day

When JoAnn and I started out we worked with a lot of buyers and it was a wonderful time. Most agents start with buyers and many never bother with sellers because sellers carry a heavier burden of responsibility. Buyers are easier. The only challenge with buyers is keeping their loyalty and being there at the end. We only had that one listing and we held it open three or four times a week. This gave us buyers to show and we did. We developed a lot of tips, myths, and secrets and we will share them here.

Frustrated with the question of what to do next we created a simple goal of three showings a day. This wasn't three houses; it was three separate prospects, and we showed them at least one house each day. Some days it was just three houses and some days it was many more. This was our only goal. Every morning I would be on the MLS computer finding houses and JoAnn would be on the phone scheduling those three showings. We weren't picky. We didn't qualify them as to motivation, capacity, and criteria like we would today. We just had the one goal. Three showings. In our first year we sold 66 homes with this rule. So even though we tell you all the things you should do, there is only one thing you *must* do, and that is show property.

The Little Things

For all we have to say about putting the client first, and it is all powerfully true, the best tools you have are kindness, respect, and courtesy. Back then, JoAnn would make every client feel comfortable. She does today. She is a master communicator and she makes every relationship personal. If a buyers' child was interested in horses, she would buy them a book on horses. JoAnn listens intently. She writes down little notes on anything handy all day long and then the next morning she puts them on action lists.

She sends small gifts, cards, and letters. She recognizes client accomplishments. She tells me it is the little things that matter and it is. JoAnn listens for what interests each client. What is their passion? What are their hobbies? What are the key things that are important to that client? It is these little things that guide JoAnn to serve them in ways only meant for them. This is putting the client first and it keeps clients and it attracts more clients.

Hot Buttons

Every client has their own priorities. What is important to one may be unimportant to the next. It may be schools or the proximity to medical facilities. Perhaps it is shopping or family and friends.

For JoAnn and me it was trees. We were looking to rent and found our home in an unattractive neighborhood of older homes on acre lots overgrown with cactus. All we had was an address and a phone number to call if we liked it. We didn't even have a key but the minute we saw the house, we wanted it. There were old courtyard walls, three tall Aleppo pines, and a dozen citrus trees in the back. We looked through the windows and said, "Oh look, it's even been updated a little," as if that were a bonus because we had already made our decision. Over the years, thanks to real estate, we wore our landlord down and bought our home. We've since built more courtyard walls and planted more trees and we will probably never move because our home pushed our hot button.

Listen to your clients. Find their hot buttons and then find the home that pushes them. If it sounds like real estate is mystical here, that's because it is. Buyers make the decision to buy during that first those 10 feet inside the front door. Give them time. Stand in the foyer and talk. Let them feel the house. If they like it, they will begin to forgive every drawback and throw their criteria away. If they don't like the home in that first ten feet, they will magnify every shortcoming. Just keep showing more homes until you walk into the one that grabs them.

Working with buyers just takes time and persistence. They are actually easy and the more you seek to serve them, the easier they are. Looking for a home is terribly exciting for a buyer. Share that excitement. Get excited with them. Now you are motivating. Questions like "Isn't this nice?" go a long way when you've found the right home.

JoAnn often says that you can't sell someone a home they don't want. People sell themselves when they find the one they want. I think the secret is sharing that experience with them. Know your stuff. Know the features, the comps, the neighborhood, and all that but knowing your client first is the key to working with buyers and selling a lot of homes.

You can do this.

Chapter 5 Summary

Buyers are clients experiencing buyer emotions.

The Empowered Client

- Technology is changing real estate.
- The dependent client model is waning.
- The super agent embraces the empowered client.

- Service is the glue.
- Buyers are looking for a house, not an agent.

The Three Cares About Your Buyer

- Motivations—Goals and dreams.
- Capacity—Qualified for a mortgage.
- Expectations—Criteria.

Finding Property

- Empowered clients make it easier.
- Know your market.
- Show all available—MLS and FSBOs.

Showing Property

- Set appointments, be courteous and punctual, gather feedback; be a good agent.
- Give them space
- Benefits versus features.
- Asking questions to learn and help buyers learn about themselves.
- Always closing—You can't sell a house but you need to let them buy. "Do you want to make an offer on this one?"

Keep Showing Property

- Criteria changes.
- Think out of the box.
- Don't give up.

Three Showings a Day

- This is what you do next.
- Make it an unbreakable rule.
- Only one thing you must do.

(*continued*)

(*continued*)

The Little Things

- Listen for opportunities.
- Make it personal.
- Put the client first.

Hot Buttons

- Everyone has one.
- Be persistent.
- Share the experience.

6

Everything You Need to Know about Working with Sellers

Sellers are clients experiencing a different set of emotions than buyers. Sellers are more difficult to work with than buyers because they have performance expectations. It is your job to get the home sold and every day you carry that burden until it closes.

Unlike the buyer who has little to lose financially if unsuccessful, the seller is consumed with the dollars. A seller has expenses. A seller more often than not has a loan and carrying costs. If they have already moved, a vacant home can become relatively expensive. Time is not on a seller's side. They feel pressures. A super agent seeks to understand.

A seller is also much more attuned to the market. To get sold they must compete against what else is on the market. They swing between fear and greed. In a rising market, a seller wants to squeeze every last penny out of the deal. In a depressed market a seller worries that they won't be able to sell. In a flat market, they don't know what to feel so their moods swing day to day.

Listers Last

Although some sellers try selling the home themselves, most feel they need help. They are looking for an agent and, when they find one, they are willing to enter into a listing agreement. Having a listing creates contractual loyalty. For this reason, agents who expect to last concentrate on sellers.

Sellers also take less time than buyers because sellers are not sitting next to you in your car. A seller may take as little as an hour to prepare, an hour to list, an hour to set up the marketing, and an hour to negotiate the deal when an offer comes in. This is a simplified example but compared to showing a buyer for months on end, it is a vast improvement.

A super agent quickly finds that they can bundle their listing activities. Marketing 50 listings does not take 50 times the time it takes to market one listing. Systems can be created so many sellers can be served well at the same time.

Most sellers are also planning to buy and this gives the listing agent an inside track to work with them as buyers. Signs on the street create buyer calls. When you hold an open house to pick up buyers, you have the added bonus of selling your listing in the process.

Listers last because representing a seller gives the super agent an opportunity to build their brand while advertising their listings. As we said in Chapter 5, buyers are easier, buyers are fun, and you may have a wonderful career in real estate without ever representing a seller, but there are only so many buyers you can serve at one time without burning the candle at both ends. Listings can be leveraged. There is no ceiling on how many sellers you may represent. JoAnn and I have carried as many as 250 listings and gotten them all sold.

We will cover how you acquire that listing inventory in Part II, but your first listing will probably come from your circle of influence or a buyer who also has a house to sell.

The Three Cares About Your Seller

There are three things you must know about your seller. You must know their:

1. Motivation: Why they are selling and where they are going?
2. Capacity: Do they have equity and how much?
3. Expectations: How much do they want and what are they looking for in an agent?

You must care about these three things or you will have no idea how to serve your seller.

"What about the property?" You ask. "Shouldn't we start with what we hope to sell?" No, you must always start with the client. Don't feel bad. Many get this confused. They think that real estate is all about the numbers, the comps, the statistics, the costs, the land, and the structures while real estate is really all about people—the clients and their emotions. A super agent knows this and devotes the majority of his or her time on feelings. This is probably why women excel in this business. It is a wonderful opportunity for both men and women, but the men must get in touch with their feminine side and understand that real estate is all about the clients.

The Listing Appointment

Having said all that, preparing for the listing appointment is all about the house. You need to research everything you can about when it was built, by whom, its past marketing history, and what other homes like it are being offered at and being sold for. You may guess at what it should sell for but resist the temptation to set a price before the appointment.

Super agents send a pre-list package because it saves time and pre-sells the client on using you. A pre-list package includes information about you, your track record, your marketing plan and so on. It can be as large or small as you deem effective. A pre-list package also serves to keep the appointment firm. Without it we experience cancellations because they already listed. With it they wait to talk to us.

Listing presentations can be prepared and practiced or they can evolve through repetition. To this day, our to-do list includes creating a better listing presentation. I tell you this to give you encouragement that there is no magic bullet and what works for you may not work for another and vice versa. I will tell you what JoAnn and I do and you can take it from there. Just remember this is an ever-evolving thing that only has a chance to evolve when you do it over and over again. If you have never done a listing presentation, then just get out there and do it awful. Then do it awful again and again until it's not so awful and somewhere along the line you'll be pretty good. Do not wait and practice until you are ready. Jump in.

The first thing we do is ring the bell, smile, and hand the client our card confirming our appointment. Then we say we want to walk around and if they want to accompany us or not, it is okay. I always have a pad and pen in my hand. A tablet device will do. I might want to take notes but I want them to see that I'm ready to do so. Rule one is to like the house. If you don't like the house, your chances of getting the listing go to zero. Besides, I've never had a house I didn't like better the minute our sign goes up. No need to gush, just be positive. Start asking questions. A super agent is a super motivator and if you expect them to hire you, you must ask a lot of questions and listen hard at the answers. Show them you care by asking about them and their situation. Be thorough. People are more relaxed walking around. Now is the time to learn all you can.

When you are ready, set the scene by suggesting the kitchen or the dining room table. If they suggest the couch or any other location, say no, you need to be at a table. Choose your chair with the light in mind. You don't want an open window backlighting anyone so you can't see faces. Always ask whether this chair is okay. You don't want to plop down in Mom or Dad's favorite spot. Your courtesy will set you apart from some agents who have preceded you.

Usually the walking-around questions lead to more questions and we start with those. Ultimately we lead into talking about our plan to sell the home. Whatever your plan, whatever your materials, there is only one thing to remember here. Exude confidence. Let your seller know that you can do the job and let them know before discussing price.

We never price the home up front. Pricing, for us, has always been a process of explaining the market, what has sold and what is for sale, and then letting the seller set the price. Some sellers will insist on a price from us first and we give our professional opinion but we point out that the home is theirs to sell and they must be comfortable with the price. "Won't sellers set too high a price out of greed?" you ask. This is true only if we failed to explain the market well. Give your client credit. It is their decision. Your role is to serve them. Your honesty, competence, and care will guide them to the right price.

We never turn down a listing over price. We tell them it is their home and they should try what they want, but we tell them if it is overpriced and immediately begin the process of getting to the right price, because a home will not sell for more than it's worth no matter what you do.

The Magic Question

JoAnn and I used to wait for the magic question. Today, we go ahead and ask it for them just to keep things moving along. The reason we call it magic is because it means they are actually considering us to list their home. The magic question is "How much do you charge?" If they don't ask, you are just there for information or to confirm their decision to go with Uncle Billy. You want this question. You want it desperately. It signals your turn at bat and when it comes, you want to knock it out of the park.

There have been books, articles, and tutorials about commissions and I want to keep it simple here because it really is. The Real Estate Settlement Procedures Act, RESPA, dictates that commission must be freely negotiable and that agents may not engage in any way to fix prices. Your commission is whatever you decide it is, but whatever your commission is, stick to it. A super agent who attains high sales numbers by offering a commission rate that does not properly cover their expenses is only kidding themselves. An agent who changes their commission at the listing table has taken the first step to ruining a beautiful relationship. The minute you negotiate with a seller you are no longer their respected real estate advisor for you have taken the first step to becoming a commodity. The client can now compare labels and look for the best price. The client can now be released from any feelings of loyalty or respect for what you do. You are now just a can of beans and the seller wants a discount coupon.

How do you get your full commission and never waiver? You say what it is with pride. You are prepared to recount all that you do to earn that commission. You say it with confidence. You exude confidence that you can sell the home. You use whatever it takes. Just do not negotiate with your seller. This is your golden moment. They have asked the magic question and if you just hang in there, the moment they are satisfied with your answer, all that remains is the paperwork.

A top luxury agent in Los Angeles told me about a client she had. She said he called her up on the phone and read her the riot act. He kept saying, "What am I paying you for?" and she was incensed. He had a long list of complaints but all she could remember was, what am I paying you for? She managed to restrain herself from telling him he hadn't paid her anything yet and she sat down to make a list of all she did. She was hot and the list was long and in the end she controlled her anger and didn't send it to him but she says she has that list to this day and it makes her a better agent. Make your own list. Write it down and make it as long as you can and keep it and add to it from time to time and the next time you discuss commission you will be stronger and you will win.

Make the Home Appealing

Congratulations, you got that listing. Now, you must get it sold. Selling your listing is a logical repeatable step-by-step process and the first step is to make it appealing. You cannot simply list the home, rush back to the office to input the MLS information, press the publish button and wait for the phone to ring. You must get the home ready. Make a list of what the home needs before it can go on sale. For some the list is short and for some it is long. Your goal here is to make it the best it can be.

We get sellers who want to know if they should remodel to improve their chances of selling. Our answer is almost always no. The minute you change the countertops the cabinets look shabby. The minute you finish the cabinets, you need new appliances, then new flooring, then the bathrooms look dated and one thing leads to another. Remodeling is a long and bumpy road better taken when you move into a home so you can enjoy the fruits of your labors. There are fixes that make sense, however, and you must advise your client of glaring deficiencies. Repair the obvious. A leaky faucet will spoil the whole showing. Paint and carpet are the two best improvements, often turning nickels into dollars, but be careful. At the end of the day, sellers feel that they must get that money back and they will want those dollars from the buyer. The more the seller can just sell what they have, the better satisfied they will be.

We prepare every home. We stage every home. We clean every home. We even wash the windows. Even a sad home suffering deferred maintenance and offered as is can benefit from a positive presentation. Cleanliness alone can send a powerful message of pride that buyers receive positively. We have a reputation for having the good listings because we work at it. Not surprisingly, we also have a reputation for getting top dollar and that is something you want to emulate because sold listings are your number one track to more listings.

Make the Home Available

Once you list the home, your real work with the seller begins. Homes that are shown sell and homes that are difficult to see take forever. Being on the market is not easy. You have to counsel your client on repairs, staging, pre-packing, and showings. Yes, they need a lockbox otherwise agents will put them at the end of the line and show their home only if they can't sell a house on lockbox first. Yes, they need to be gone when buyers are looking at the house. Buyers engage sellers to explore their motivation. They want to know how solid the price is. Any time your seller opens their mouth with a buyer, your seller is either making a disclosure or a promise and you want disclosures to be in writing and promises to be negotiated. They must be absent. Cats can hide but dogs must be gone as well.

Make the Home Famous

Now you can put it on MLS. Now you can tell the world how wonderful your listing is. What you do from here is up to you. Many agents subscribe to the idea that any listing properly priced will sell by virtue of being on the MLS alone. MLS listings get picked up by aggregators such as Realtor.com, Trulia.com, and Zillow.com. The key here is that the listing be properly priced. These agents do not believe a listing can be sold quicker or for more money by doing more.

JoAnn and I agree with proper pricing but we also believe that the proper price can be moved upward with advertising and marketing. The greater the exposure, the greater the chances of more than one buyer being interested, and any time you have more than one buyer the price goes up. A quality brochure elevates a property. Buyers look at five or ten homes and at the end of the day, the only thing they have to remember them by are the flyers they collected along the way. Advertised open houses are busier open houses and busy open houses inspire a sense of buyer panic as they look at all the other people looking at the home they like. A virtual tour becomes a digital tool for the buyer to get approval from family and friends. A broker tour increases the chances of finding that agent who likes the house and starts showing all her prospects the good deal she found. These are just a few of the added tools available to sell your listing.

Communicate with Your Seller

Your seller anguishes every day they go unsold and you are the only one who can ease their pain. When you think of it this way, you will keep your seller informed.

Ask for feedback on showings and report it to your seller. There are systems for this ranging from the showing agent leaving their business card for you to collect to digital solutions that e-mail the showing agent and then e-mail both you and your client. Work the feedback. Look for guidance and trends. You may not be able to get rid of a busy street but you can certainly suggest painting an offending purple wall.

Finding the Right Price

Your seller's original asking price may not work and your seller may become fixated on that price. They may look for any reason other than price for the home not selling. But if it is the price, you must step up and tell them. The last thing you want a seller to do is languish on the market. You must find the right price.

Sellers often find reducing worrisome and you will have to develop your answers to those worries. Here are a few.

Reducing the price introduces the home to a new audience of buyers. Everyone searching homes on a computer must enter a price range. If the top number of their search is just under your price, they never see you.

Can't they make an offer? Yes, but if the gap between what you are asking and what they want to pay is too great, they will have no confidence of success and move on. Plus, buyers tend to offer lower than where they want to end up which only makes the gap bigger. The closer you get to what a buyer perceives as the right price, the better the initial offers become.

Shouldn't we fix something or offer an allowance? We can, but we made those decisions when we got the home ready. I once had a seller say to me, "We haven't had a showing in 60 days, should I replace the carpet?" It's okay to read that again. I remember shaking the cobwebs from my head and then I explained that the lack of showings was the problem and a price reduction would be the solution. Without showings you have nothing.

You must help your seller find the right price. Without the right price you have no offers and without an offer you are just marketing. One last word on price. Time does not work in a seller's favor. I get sellers who say, "I'm not in a hurry. I can wait for my price." When you hear this the problem is probably motivation more than price, but point out that the longer you are on the market the more likely you are to receive lower offers. On a fresh listing an agent may advise their buyer to make a better offer just because the listing is new. On an old listing the agent will say, "Try what you like, they've been on the market a long time."

Be There at the End

Don't disregard that unmotivated seller. One morning they will call and say things have changed and they want to get sold right now. That seller who refused to reduce will ultimately come down to meet the market. Maybe your listing hasn't sold because of market changes. Get your seller to go with the market or just wait and the market will swing back. The thing is, you want to do your very best for your client and you want to be there when they sell. Keep that client by putting them first. Give them complete honesty and they will stay with you. Be totally competent in all you do and they will not go elsewhere. Care about them, their needs, and their goals, and you will stick together as two peas in a pod.

Communicate with your sellers. JoAnn and I have never had a situation made worse by meeting face to face with a client. Ask questions and listen to the answers. Believe in solutions and keep the client.

Patience

All good things come to those who wait. I had a seller call the other day looking for some gimmick to sell the house. I knew he was a sportsman and I said, "Sometimes you just have to have the patience to fish." I went on to explain that you might decide to go fishing and you put together a plan. You put together the best equipment. You hire the best guide, you go to the best spot, and at some point you have to just fish and sometimes the fish are just not biting. I went on to explain that for any given week or even month, for that matter, there may not even be a buyer looking in your neighborhood and your price range. Yes, you can reduce your price until the greedy bargain hunters come out of the woodwork, but sometimes it is just best to fish. He understood and we waited.

I want to make a couple of points about that exchange. First of all, I knew this client. We had talked before. I knew he fished. This example may have never worked on another client. Second of all, there is a time to push and there is a time to wait. You cannot press and force everything. Sometimes homes have to sell when the time is right, when that right buyer comes to town. Be there for your client. Take on their anguish and relieve their pain. Never give up and be sure you are there when it sells.

Chapter 6 Summary

Listers Last

- Contractual loyalty.
- Bundle activities.
- Buyers come to you.

(*continued*)

(*continued*)

The Three Cares About Your Seller

- Why are they selling?
- How much is their equity?
- What are they looking for in an agent?

The Listing Appointment

- Pre-list package.
- Walking through.
- At the table.

The Magic Question

- How much do you charge?
- Never waiver.
- List what they are paying you for.

Selling the Home

- Make the home appealing.
- Make the home available.
- Make the home famous.

Communicate with Your Seller

- Finding the right price.
- Be there at the end.
- Be patient.

7 The *ABCs* of Making a Deal

I t is true that not every deal can be made. A worse truth, however, is that deals that can and should be put together, don't get done. Spouses, lawyers, friends, relatives, buyers, and sellers kill deals and yes, agents kill deals, too. The good news is that you don't have to be that agent. The even better news is that you can help and keep others from being deal killers.

You can be a super agent and super agents don't break deals, they make them. This difference alone probably accounts for half the income disparity between super agents and the rest of our profession. Imagine, just by making deals like a super agent you may double your income. Double. So let's think a little about why deals get done and why they don't.

Deals that cannot be made are a result of one or more party having unreasonable demands or expectations. Absent unreasonableness, most deals are doable. This is wonderful news. This means your challenge does not lie in trying to change the unchangeable facts, or moving the property to a different location, or adding on or taking away from the structures. Your job is to just get the parties to be reasonable. This is doable.

The Three Secret Ingredients to Making a Deal

So, how do you achieve reasonableness? How do you make this happen when you don't even have influence on the other side? For that matter, you often don't have influence on your own client. Clients have free will. They can be arrogant, timid, pushy, nice, mean, and any other emotional expression they wish. Good, bad, or ugly, it is your job to represent their best interests and to put their goals first. This may seem impossible but super agents know that reasonableness can be found and that almost all deals can be made. They know this because they know the secret ingredients. They know how to achieve reasonableness.

Secret Ingredient 1. To promote reasonableness, you must always be reasonable. You can never be stubborn, stand on principle, get offended, or be angry.

You must be the model for cool, calm, and collected. We have seen agents do all of these things against the best interests of their clients. They send long e-mails and you can always judge their emotional state by the length of the e-mail, or the use of all CAPS or the lack of paragraph breaks. They talk on the phone forever. They go on without pausing for breath. They are everything except reasonable and the only response that can get them where you want them to be is calm. If you have any hope of getting them there, you must be what you want them to be.

Secret Ingredient 2. You must be resolute in your belief that a deal can be made. There are agents who lose deal after deal by identifying offers as low or otherwise without hope. A super agent believes a deal can always be made. They know that reasonableness will find its way into the situation. A super agent's belief is like a magnet attracting reasonableness and bringing the parties together.

Secret Ingredient 3. You must never give up. The thing about unreasonableness is that it has a limited battery life. Sooner or later unmotivated clients become motivated. Sooner or later, whatever it is that is sucking the life out of a deal gives up and succumbs to reasonableness and belief and not giving up.

JoAnn is a master deal maker because she is the master of these three secret ingredients. She treats every client with total calm and respect. She always believes a deal can be made and she never throws in the towel. We had a fellow from Chicago offer $550,000 on an $899,000 listing and 73 days later we had a deal at $640,000. Yes, the seller was overpriced and the buyer was outwardly indifferent and a lot took place in the interim, but JoAnn never lost her calm, and never lost her belief and never gave up.

Tips on Turning Simple into Easy

If this seems simplified, it is. Deal making really is that simple. Please note, we did not say easy. Easy is not necessarily simple and vice versa.

Staying calm can be very difficult. Believing can challenge your perception of reality. Never giving up can be tedious. To make the simple easy, we offer a few tips.

Tip A. Put your client first. This is their deal, not yours. Yes, their goals should become your goals, but you need to be their champion, not their foil. Be strong for your clients. No matter where they are on the reasonableness scale, you must be reasonable for them. Do not reflect them. Serve them by being the best that they can be.

Tip B. Never judge or attempt to insert your opinion in order to manipulate. If your client asks what you think they should do, or what would you do, or what would a higher intelligence advise, then offer a positive path to reasonableness. Never offer negative opinions about the other party's motives. Put your client first by trusting the truth, being honest, and keeping to the facts.

Tip C. Motivate with questions. Asking questions of your client or the other agent is the quickest route to their self-realization. Asking the right question at the right time often helps the other person think things out. What is the right question and when is the right time? You may never know. Just keep asking in a reasonable and calm tone and you are bound to get it right sooner or later.

Tip D. Stay detached from the outcome. There is a truism which says that the more detached you remain from the outcome, the more attached the outcome becomes to you. You see it every day. Scared money never wins in Las Vegas. People unprepared to walk away settle for less. Detachment doesn't mean not caring about the outcome. It just takes the desperation out of the deal. Being detached for an attached client is sometimes the greatest service you bring to the table.

Tip E. Acceptance. When you realize that some deals work and some deals don't, when you get to the point where you realize that deals happen as they are supposed to, that's when all the deals that should work do. Deal making is often a matter of just not messing it up. We've seen many deals go south because one or the other or both parties go against their desires over some small thing that in retrospect was stupid and cost them what they wanted.

Does this idea of acceptance fly in the face of calm, belief, and determination? Not at all. Many deals that should happen, that are supposed to happen, don't happen for lack of reasonableness, and for disbelief and for not keeping on. But as super agents we know we did our best. We do our best to achieve reasonableness in others but we are not always successful. We maintain our belief but others may not. We don't give up but others do and no matter how resolute we are these deals do not make it. Acceptance gives us peace and hope and here's the kicker; we believe there are no dead deals, only deals that haven't happened yet.

Out of more than 5,000 home sales you would be surprised at how many were resurrected months or even years later. Once people decide to sell, they will eventually get sold. Once people decide to buy, they will ultimately take the plunge.

Write Offers That Win Acceptance

Let's get specific. When representing a buyer your goal is to write an offer. More accurately, your goal is to write an offer that has hopes of being accepted and that depends on the reasonableness of your buyer. Getting your buyer from "I want to write an offer" to "I want to write a winning offer" occurs in the land of important knowledge and accurate information. You need to dig for everything you can about the property and the seller's motivations and you need to share it all with your buyer. It is their decision what price and terms to offer and they need to make it an informed decision. Here are a few things you and your buyer need to know about the seller and the property.

- How long has the seller been on the market? A longer period could signal an initial stubbornness or a current willingness to deal.
- What was their starting price and have they reduced?
- Were they listed before and failed to sell?

All this and much more may be researched on the MLS.

Call the listing agent and get more information. Always start by asking if the property is still available. If your buyer cannot have this particular dream home, the earlier you know the better. Your second question should be your least significant and you always want to have insignificant questions. Maybe your buyer wants to know how long ago the seller replaced the air conditioner or if the pool has ever been acid washed. If your buyer has no insignificant question, make up one of yours, such as did the sellers complete a pre-inspection or do they already have a home warranty? The importance of a soft Q and A is to build rapport gradually, find out how knowledgeable the listing agent is, and hopefully get them to drop their guard for the more insightful questions such as have they had any other offers or what is their timetable for moving.

Find out as much as you can but keep your questions relevant. You may be talking to another super agent who wants to make a deal or you may be talking to a newbie. Either way, you must respect their representation and avoid such bonehead questions as how motivated are the sellers, why are they selling or how much will they really take.

Run comparable listings (comps) on the MLS and share with your buyer what other homes have sold for, what other homes are on the market, and what homes are currently pending. A word about comps: only so much can be inferred from what has happened with other homes between other buyers and other sellers. Regardless of the comps, this deal is going to be what your buyer is willing to pay and what this seller is willing to take. We get buyers who believe that a seller must take a certain number because that is what the comps say. This is untrue. A seller may do as they please. It is their property. Be sure you present comps with this caveat. Sometimes you must repeat this over and over again.

Get the House

Of course, comps, days on market, and everything else go out the window if there is another offer. Any good agent will share this fact with you. Some will even give you the competing terms but most will not. Now you must ask your buyer to truly examine their desire for the property, because if they want it badly you must do everything you can to get it for them.

Bear in mind that there are many terms other than price that may get your buyer the deal. Ask the other agent for guidance. Ask what is important to the seller.

We had a buyer, a long-time client on what must have been their sixth purchase with us, who wanted this home very much. The listing agent had three other offers and we needed an edge. We went back to view the home and the elderly sellers were there. They were very nice and during the conversation we learned that their biggest challenge was going to be emptying the house as they were going to assisted living. We went back to our office and countered a provision that the buyers would arrange for an estate sale and pay the fees. Our buyer got the deal.

Remember, your buyer has entrusted you with getting them what they want. Be their champion. Want it for them. Be honest, competent, calm, and full of belief to keep it going. Ask questions because they motivate. Questions help others to move in the right direction. Questions give your client guidance. And communicate. You must keep your buyer, who is on pins and needles, constantly informed. You must keep the other agent up to speed. We can't tell you how many times we've represented a seller and a buyer's agent failed to keep us informed about their buyer and ended up losing the sale to another buyer who came along in the meantime. Communicate. Get through. Confirm receipt of the message. Write a winning offer and make that deal.

Presenting Offers to Your Seller

Nothing beats getting an offer on your listing. It is a thrill. All your hard work has been justified. Now you have something to bring your seller. How you present that offer, will have a great deal to do with whether or not you ultimately make a deal. Let's examine the elements of a successful presentation.

You start with confirming receipt of the offer with the buyer's agent. This is so basic, yet agents fail in this simple step all the time and in doing so they miss a huge opportunity. Your seller is going to ask you about the buyer. They want to know if it's the couple with the twins or the ones who have Mom living with them. They want to know if they are local or from out of town. They want to know and so do you. Call the other agent and get all you can. Is this a new client for this agent or is it someone they've worked with before? Work up to the important questions, like how motivated are they to get this house, because this is information you can use when advising your seller.

Next, you notify your seller. How you communicate the news with your seller is something you should have already discussed with your seller when you listed the property. Put a note or reminder in the listing file. Whatever medium you use, text, e-mail, voicemail, or phone contact, you need to be specific and say you have an offer. Saying only that you need to reach them is no good. They must know an offer exists as soon as possible.

How you choose to describe or not describe the offer is very important and you should tailor your decision to how well you know the seller and the terms of the offer. If it is a low offer, for example, and you know the sellers to be reactionary, you might preview before stating the amount that it is low with an encouraging word such as it is a good place to start. For another client you may withhold mentioning the lowness of the offer to build anticipation and avoid early dismissal. This is where we get back to all real estate is about people and emotions, and you should seek to understand your clients. This is one of the cares of sellers: know their expectations.

Do not make the mistake of thinking a clean, full-price offer is a done deal and just spill the beans. We've seen many such offers scare a seller. Moving is suddenly a reality. Maybe they didn't ask enough. Treat every offer carefully and present it with an understanding of your seller's motivations.

It does not matter whether you present the offer face to face or through e-mail. What does matter is that you let them absorb the offer and the terms. Answer their questions without offering advice. Give them an opportunity to accept the offer. This is what you would want another agent to do with your buyer's offer and you should do the same. Give your seller this opportunity to accept. It shows respect. It is always their decision.

Always Counter?

If your seller does not accept, you should always advise countering rather than rejecting. Rejecting an offer is the first step toward unreasonableness and countering is the first step toward a meeting of the minds. Always counter. In fact, there is a school of thought that advises always countering even when the offer is acceptable to your seller. Bear in mind that there is a danger here. The moment you counter, the ball is in the buyer's court. They can then accept, reject, or counter. They have no obligation to counter back. Their agent may be unable to advise against rejection and the deal is lost. Buyers can be quirky. They fall in love with your seller's house and the first bump in the road, it is like a breakup and they make an offer on another house on the rebound. On the other hand, we have had buyers displeased with an immediate acceptance, thinking they offered too high.

We believe it is best to counter if only to clarify the intent of the parties on terms. After all, if the deal is so shaky that the other side cannot deal with a soft counter, it is best to know now rather than later when your seller is in escrow and losing market exposure.

Now would be a good time to discuss putting together a good, clear contract that spells out the intent of the parties. Intent is an important concept. As an agent you must seek clarity even though others may seek ambiguity or language that is subject to interpretation.

Most of all, understand this, contracts do not improve after the signatures. Get it right up front. If this means having the courage to advise your client to counter when it may lose the deal, so be it, and be sure to tell them the risks. It is their decision. Tell them the risks of not countering and the risks of countering and leave it to them. Trust the truth and accept that not all deals happen unless they are supposed to.

The rewards of becoming a deal maker are huge. The thrill of making a deal is addictive. We are addicts. It doesn't matter if it is a multimillion-dollar mansion or a mobile home affixed to a piece of land, we are hooked on the deal. Bringing the parties together and knowing that, were it not for you, the deal may not have happened is an experience that goes far beyond the monetary reward. As JoAnn and I drive through neighborhoods we point at homes and say we sold that one and that one—it is like an elixir.

Deal making will keep you young. You can do this.

Chapter 7 Summary

Not Every Deal Can Be Made

- You don't have to be a deal killer.
- Double your income by being a deal maker.
- Just get the parties to be reasonable.

The Three Secret Ingredients

- Promote reasonableness by being reasonable.
- Believe a deal can be made.
- Never give up.

Tips on Turning Simple into Easy

- Put your client first and be strong for them.
- Never judge or insert you opinion.
- Motivate with questions.
- Stay detached from the outcome.
- Accept that deals happen as they are supposed to.

Write Offers That Win Acceptance

- Get information from the MLS.
- Get information from the seller's agent.
- Run the comps.

Get the House

- Other offers?
- What is important to the seller?
- Communicate with all parties.

Presenting Offers to Your Seller

- Confirm receipt.
- Notify your seller.
- Take care in how you phrase presentation.

Always Counter?

- There are risks.
- Buyers have no obligation to counter back.
- Better to know now if the deal is shaky.

The rewards of becoming a deal maker go beyond just money.

8 Contract to Closing

We often tell clients that we are only halfway there when the deal is made. Getting from contract to close is a treacherous trip and you will need all the help you can muster to get to your destination.

Super agents know this and they respect the process and they close most of their transactions. We didn't say *all* their transactions because the truth is not all transactions close. There are just too many variables involved, too many people, and too many things that can go wrong. But just as the super agent makes more deals by virtue of not killing them, a super agent closes more transactions by staying connected to the process and their client.

Each state has its own laws and rules about contract to close. Some jurisdictions require the services of an attorney while others do not. Some states separate the seller of title insurance from the escrow officer while others do not. Some states dictate a judicial-foreclosure process while others allow a trustee-sale process. For our purposes we will concentrate only on your role in representing the client through the escrow process as it is commonly defined and executed. Check your state laws for specifics.

Escrow

The first thing to do after making a deal is for the buyer's agent to open escrow. The function of escrow is to have an independent third party gather all parties' documents and monies together and, when ready, record the transfer of ownership in the property and disburse funds. The parties include but are not limited to the buyer, seller, their respective agents, the lender for the new loan, the appraiser, lien holders who must be paid, homeowner associations, issuers of title insurance, inspectors, attorneys if required or desired, and others. As you can see, escrow is organized chaos. The escrow officer is beholden to no one and is bound only by the initial escrow instructions or the contract given at opening of escrow.

A Super Agent's Role

It amazes us at how many agents hand their clients off to this process and just wait for their check. They reason that everyone wants the deal to close so they just get out of the way. Many of these untended clients do get closed but almost as many of these clients fall out of escrow over issues that could have been resolved.

A super agent knows this and takes an active role representing their client throughout the process. As a result, a super agent closes more transactions than the average agent. When you consider all this, it is a wonder that the average agent does five deals a year.

This active role begins with opening or creating a file and a checklist of all the steps to be performed. Timelines must be tracked constantly. The escrow file should include an information sheet with all the contact information in one place.

The first thing a super agent does is to insert themselves into the process by notifying all parties that they will be representing their buyer through the escrow process. Now is the time to set expectations. If you are attending all inspections—and we recommend you do—say so. If you represent the seller and plan to be there for all property visits, say so. If you are leaving the lockbox on or taking it off, say so. You must assert yourself or you will get lost in the shuffle. It is in your client's best interest for you to control the escrow process.

Representing the Seller

There are buyers and buyer's agents who do not realize that the home is not yet theirs and especially in the case of a vacant home, they come and go at will. Do not allow this. Your seller has exposure and liability. Require that you be notified of all visits. To ensure this we remove the lockbox as soon as we have a deal. This does not make us popular with some agents who would prefer free access, but we are not in business to be popular we are in business to represent our client. As a consequence, we never experience a home inspection we are not aware of and we never hear about an appraiser after he has come and gone. We do have the added burden of dealing with access requests but it better serves our client, so we do it. As to being popular, most agents now respect our removing the lockbox and emulate us.

When you represent the seller, you must help them disclose everything they know so that they walk away with no lingering issues. Document these disclosures in writing. Whether it is a government form or an e-mail confirming what was said, you want to paper it well. Documentation is the best protection for both you and your client.

You must seek surety of closing for your seller. Ultimately, your seller must vacate the home and this usually includes plans to rent or buy, both of which require commitments in the form of deposits and occupancy dates. Your seller needs surety of closing in order to make those plans and commitments. To attain this surety you must shut the doors in the contract. Doors are contingencies or escape clauses through which a buyer may get out of a contract and it is your job to document the fulfillment of every contingency.

You must shut the doors. You do this by staying on top of the buyer's agent and asking questions. Call the lender every day if you have to. Verify the buyer's source of funds and then reverify. Stay on top of timelines. Send reminders. Requests for extensions are red flags. Ask why. Problems in escrow usually start small and early detection is your best hope for a cure.

When representing your seller, you must stay in constant communication with the buyer's agent to be sure they are driving the deal. It is the buyer who must obtain financing. It is the buyer who must bring in the money. It is the buyer who must sign off on the inspections. As the seller's agent you must rely on that buyer and that buyer's agent to perform. You may be dealing with a super agent and you may not. A super agent will appreciate your communication and a not-so-super agent will need your urging.

Representing the Buyer

If you are the buyer's agent, you must be the driver of the deal. Your buyer will have many things to provide to the lender. Communicate. Remind your buyer. Ask what you can do to help. Keep the process urgent and moving.

You must control the due diligence or inspection period. Your buyer has a limited time to get many things done and you must keep them on track. You must tell your client to schedule everything through you so that you are aware of each step's completion.

Protect your buyer's earnest deposit and alert your buyer any time their money is at risk. It is always their decision but it is your responsibility to keep them informed of any and all decisions to be made. Time is of the essence in a contract, which means there are timelines and deadlines that must be met. Miss a deadline and your buyer may be stuck with a deal they end up not wanting or, worse yet, they end up losing their deposit.

Your job is to track the timelines and keep your buyer's options and contingencies open for as long as possible. A buyer's situation changes every day. They may get their financing easily or they may have a hundred hoops to jump through before they get out of underwriting. They may have no problem with their down payment or they may have to go to plan B or plan C for the money. They may have remorse, split up, or decide to go to Tahiti and paint. You must keep their options open. They may find out things about the property that change their desire. They may have a reasonable seller over repairs and they may not. You must serve and protect them, sometimes even from themselves, and you must treat all parties fairly.

The idea of keeping your buyer's cancellation options open may seem counterproductive. We know agents who make every effort to tie their buyer down so they can't walk from a deal. They recommend more earnest money than necessary. They advise their buyers to agree when asked for nonrefundable earnest money. They want the deal to close so they can get paid. Don't be that guy. Don't be that woman. You need to put your client first and keep their options open. After all, the seller's agent is trying to shut those doors, representing your client may include treating that seller's agent fairly but it does not include helping her at your client's expense.

Dual Agency

After reading all that, how can an agent possibly represent both the buyer and the seller? Some states just do not allow it. We are in Arizona and we have done dual-agency deals. On the plus side, the other agent is very nice. Our seller doesn't have to worry about the deal being driven because we are at the wheel. Negotiating with yourself can be smooth as silk. Earning two commissions is tempting. But it is not an easy path. We have a dual-agency disclosure form that spells out our duties and holds us to a much higher standard, but all that is easier said than done.

Early on, our broker explained it this way. You either get both sides in a room at the same time or you imagine the absent party there and be sure you don't say anything you don't think both sides can hear. She also said to paper it well.

The trouble comes when the deal doesn't close. How do you go after your buyer's earnest money for your seller? How do you explain what went wrong when you were the one taking care of things? We have done this, but it is not easy.

As a listing agent, we represent sellers and we often show prospects our own listings. We also hold open houses and unrepresented buyers walk in the door. Were we to not show our own listings or were we to shoo these unrepresented buyers away saying they should go find an agent, we would be going against the best interests of our seller. So we show them and we write dual-agency contracts.

Here are a few tips on serving both sides. Let the paperwork rule. Write the offer the buyer wants to write, prepare the counter the seller wants to counter, and do not advise either party. When asked, reply that you cannot advise them. Explain that dual representation is limited representation and that you may only preside over the proceedings. If they still want just you, then proceed with caution and repeated disclosure. Be sure they not only sign the dual-agency consent form but that they understand it as well.

Anticipation and Expectations

A successful closing begins and ends with anticipation and managing expectations. Whichever side you represent, it is up to you to keep everything on track. Escrow can be a very self-centered process for many participants. The termite inspector is only concerned with doing his job and turning in a report. The lender just wants to make the loan and often does not care if the deal closes timely.

Our most memorable delayed closing was a sweetheart deal that went sour in a flash. Our buyers were both dentists, total professionals, and the wife had been the essence of cool but when the moving truck was parked in the street and the key was not forthcoming, she sat at the curb and cried. Their lender, who we had recommended highly, didn't have some last piece of paperwork and when JoAnn called, he said, "Wednesday, Thursday what difference does it make?" We changed lenders that day and from that day to this, none of our clients have found themselves in tears. This is not to say every lender has closed timely but every lender has known to keep us informed so that we could anticipate and adjust for the inevitable changes.

We manage expectations by taking care to never promise that which we cannot be 100 percent sure we can deliver. We stay ahead of the process and always advise our clients of potential problems. You can tell a client ahead of time that a coming thunderstorm is a hazard, so when lighting strikes and the structure burns to the ground, the client will be okay. But if you fail to warn of a one-day delay in closing until the morning of the closing, your client will vilify you to anyone who will listen.

You see, closing is the culmination of all your efforts and if something goes wrong at the end, you are toast.

JoAnn loves to tell this story. Every day at 9 a.m. you hear a knock on the door and when you open it a nice gentleman hands you a crisp 20 dollar bill. This goes on for months and then one morning you open the door and the gentleman slaps you in the face and walks away. What do you remember, the stack of twenties or the single slap?

Anticipate and communicate. These are the secrets to a successful closing.

Until Jenny got pregnant three times in succession, she was our finest transaction coordinator. This was Jenny's secret weapon. At the end of every day she e-mailed or voicemailed every buyer and every seller who she had not otherwise communicated with that day. She had 30 to 40 of these contacts and it took her maybe a half hour. And here's the secret; even if nothing happened that day on our client's transaction file, she told them just that. Jenny knew that escrow was a fearful experience for the client and she didn't want them to worry or lose sleep. Jenny's children are in school now and we still hear compliments from past clients on how much they appreciated Jenny's daily kindness.

You may only have one escrow at a time or dozens, but you can do this. Stay on top of things and keep your client informed.

Assistance

Your broker may offer some kind of transaction assistance or you may be on your own. You may choose to do everything yourself or you may hire a freelance escrow coordinator, but do not expect them to care for your clients. You must be the reassuring voice.

There are a number of transaction-management software programs that put this all on a computer, but you are still your client's lifesaver. Remember that what you get when you computerize a mess is a faster mess. You must be organized before you seek timesavers.

We still use the Top Producer software brand because we started with them more than 14 years ago and we are familiar with the program. At a mastermind meeting of 20 top super agents we once talked software and the most impressive thing I learned was how diverse the group was. Only one other agent used Top Producer and only a couple of other brands had two users. Bottom line, they are all good or as good as you make them. We do recommend you put your escrows on a computer but when you do, remember that the device may remind you to call but it takes *you* to pick up the phone.

You can do this. You can be a super agent. You can have fewer deals fall out of escrow. Just stay engaged and stay on top of everything.

Chapter 8 Summary

Contract to Closing

- Not all transactions close.
- A super agent closes more.
- Check your state laws.

Escrow

- Independent third party.
- Many parties, many interests.
- Some agents disconnect.

A Super Agent's Role

- Open the file.
- Assert yourself.
- Set expectations and control the process.

(*continued*)

(continued)

Representing the Seller

- Control access.
- Encourage full disclosure.
- Seek surety of closing.
- Shut the doors, document fulfilled contingencies.
- Stay on top of the buyer's agent.

Representing the Buyer

- Drive the deal.
- Protect your buyer's earnest money.
- Keep you buyer's options open.

Dual Agency

- Check your state's laws.
- Proceed with caution.
- Let the paperwork rule.

Anticipation and Expectations

- Early detection solves problems.
- Communicate even if nothing has happened.
- Stay on top of things.

Assistance

- Your broker.
- Freelance help.
- Software.

9

Keeping Your Client after the Sale

An agent once asked JoAnn for her best advice to get her business back on track. This agent was experienced and she had sold maybe ten deals a year for quite a while. She concentrated on buyers. We were negotiating a deal with her and had just dropped by her house with some paperwork. She and JoAnn were standing in the open garage, having just exited the kitchen via the laundry room. I was standing on the driveway listening to the exchange.

JoAnn asked, "Where are all your transaction files?" In Arizona we are required to keep paperwork for five years after closing.

The agent pointed at the far corner of her garage. There stood a stack of five or six cardboard storage boxes. She said, "Right there."

JoAnn said, "Well, the first thing you want to do is put all those past clients on a database so you can get in touch with them."

Horror crossed her face and she raised both hands in protest. "Oh, I don't ever want to talk to those people again."

We laughed all the way home, but today it is deeply sad. This lady was terribly attractive, lived in a fine home, drove a nice car, and was very articulate. She always had a client or two working and made a fine living. But every day she had to get up and start all over again.

After maybe 20 years in the business she had nothing except for her current escrow and the expectation of a check when it closed. We had only been in the business a couple of years and already we had past clients calling with a new need or a friend who they wanted us to care for.

Better Than Social Security

The amazing thing about this business is the repeat business. We had no idea. At first glance one would assume a grocer might have repeat customers but a real estate agent? How often do people move? Maybe they relocate every 5 or 10 years. Some people live in the same house for 20 or 30 years. Besides, a lot of sellers move away. How can you build a repeat business on that?

You can and you should because it is better than social security. If all you do is close five deals a year and you keep those clients, at the end of 20 years you will have 100 faithful clients sending you business. If only 5 percent call you each year with a new need or a friend, you will have a permanent flow of the easiest and best kind of business there is. Past clients already trust you. They expect to be well served. You can now retire and do as much business working maybe 20 days a year as you did when you were working full time with new clients. Just think, you can make as much money year after year just by keeping those past clients after the sale.

Now, and I want you to be careful here, you are holding a book on being a super agent. Make sure you are sitting down. Super agents do not settle for five deals a year. Super agents have super powers. Super agents put their clients first. Super agents are super motivators and super communicators. Super agents are professionals and treat their practice as a business. Super agents are deal makers and super agents get their deals through escrow and closed. Can you imagine how much business a super agent has coming in the door from past clients? Can you feel how that massive force of goodwill grows making each year more productive and easier? All because super agents keep their clients forever and so can you.

Build a Database

All it takes is a few short years in this business and you will never struggle again. Back in Chapter 3 we told you the story of our first sale and how last year we sold our 102nd home from that past-client trail. How do we know this? We know because we put our clients on a database after our first 50 or so closings. The software is called Access and even though it is old we just keep adding clients. Our database is like owning a gold mine and every day we get fresh ore.

Our client records include every time we have touched the client, every time we have mailed them, every gift we've given them, and every referral they have brought to us. We have their children's and pet's names and anything else important to know about them. We hear from some several times a year and others every few years, but there are very few who haven't called from time to time. We add to this repository every day and use it to touch our clients several times a year.

There are many database or customer relations management (CRM) software programs on the market and they are all good. If your practice is small you can probably put all your clients on Outlook until you need a bigger program. Outlook is your e-mail program in Microsoft office. It may come with your computer so you could already have it. When you become a super agent, buy the best software you can find. Don't worry that something better may come out next month, just take the plunge and save those past clients. All software is only as good as you make it.

Return on Investment

Each year we spend between $12 and $15 per client with half that being our annual Christmas ornament. They are handmade doors and each year is a different door. It began because we had a tagline that said behind every door is an adventure. So we created a different theme each year. We've done a Dickens door, a bunkhouse door, and a Hawaiian door. Our clients love it and they save them. We now have clients send us photos of their tree with all their doors.

It is a huge effort that begins in February. JoAnn decides on this year's design and our ornament makers develop a prototype that involves a lot of FedExing back and forth. By April, production has begun and by October the ornaments begin arriving. Our team puts together boxes at their desks between phone calls and we start producing labels from our database. Then our elves personalize each ornament with the family name as they pack them all for shipping. The last boxes go in the mail by December 10th and we all breathe a sigh of relief.

This effort brings us joy and it brings us business. All year we have people mentioning their ornaments. They thank us. They can't believe it has their name on it. They return with their real estate needs and they bring their friends.

What is the return on investment you ask? On average, 5 percent of your past clients will return business to you each year. We do better than that but let's use this number. Five percent is one out of 20 clients and if you multiply the $15 we spend times 20, you will get $300 per new or returning client. In a business where the average commission is $6,000, that is a good return and you can imagine how these numbers can change with a better return or a higher average commission.

An important point here is that we make an investment in our past client relationships. You might prefer to invest your time and call them from time to time. You might choose a newsletter or any one of a hundred ways to keep in touch, but the thing is you must make an investment in keeping connected to your past clients.

The Early Days

It wasn't always like this, with thousands of ornaments going out the door. We started modestly. Our first Christmas in the business we found a deal at a kitchen store on pewter scoops, such as what you find on the bulk-foods aisle at a healthy supermarket. They were large and hadn't sold and we bought them on sale. Then we bought cookies and put five in each scoop along with some pretty tissue. We then surrounded the whole thing with cellophane from Costco and tied it with raffia. That's the ugly string that looks like dried grass. We attached a card from a box, also from Costco, and we delivered every one. There were less than 50 and it was a wonderful time.

Some of our best times came from those early years. On Valentine's Day we sent heart balloons and on the Fourth of July we gave flags. We did silly things at Halloween and always sent a card at Thanksgiving.

These were not real estate things because we treated our past clients like family. We still do.

Our second Christmas we found a great buy on a silver platter at an outlet mall. We bought all they had and travelled as far as an outlet mall in Palm Springs, California, in order to have enough for our clients. Year three we caught Costco early in September when their Christmas items came in. We bought a Santa's Workshop at a how-can-they-do-this price and personalized each one with the family name. Looking for a way to mail because the delivery list was getting too big, the next year we bought Christmas doormats that could be rolled and inserted into a tube. The next year we started the ornaments.

These early items cost more and took more time but, let me tell you, the return on investment was stupendous. Enjoy every day. Give your time when you have it and give your personalized sentiment when you must scale and economize.

Sentiments

We have never given anything to a client without a sentiment. That first year the Christmas cards came from Costco and the sentiment was already printed and we signed each one. All the rest we have written ourselves.

One year we wrote a silly thing about selling an old man's house at the North Pole. One Thanksgiving we told the story of a buyer's first Thanksgiving and how the neighbor, Mrs. Hantas, first name Poca, brought food over. It was corny but it was from our hearts and our clients loved it.

If you want to keep clients for life, treat them like family. Be sincere. Tell them how much you appreciate them and the opportunity to serve them. Do not be afraid to let down your barriers and do not let your fear of writing something sentimental hold you back. We are not going to suggest here that if you cannot write something yourself, hire it out. No. You must write it yourself. You must find in your own heart a place for your clients. Don't be that lady who said I don't ever want to talk to those people again. Open your heart and your past clients will fill it.

Closing Gifts

The first opportunity to say thank you is at a successful closing. Every two weeks JoAnn sits down with Toni, our historian and database whiz, and decides who gets a closing gift. We give a gift to our client, of course, and we give a gift to the other agent and if the lender or title officer did a particularly good job, we might gift them as well. JoAnn dictates a personal note for each gift and Toni mails them. JoAnn has done this since our first transaction. She didn't have Toni then. I was the one taking dictation but we were consistent and we were grateful because you don't succeed alone. The gifts have been a succession of wonderful little things.

A few years ago we were Christmas shopping at Tiffany's and JoAnn was struck with the beauty and affordability of their crystal line. She struck a deal with the manager and we have given weave bowls ever since. They come in that blue box with a white ribbon and people are always so flattered to receive such a fine piece. Not everyone gets a Tiffany bowl but our clients do, so they know how we feel and they stay with us.

Do not skimp on your closing gift. It may be the most important gift you give this year. This client will return. This client will bring their mother, brother, sister, or daughter. Tell them thank you.

Staying in Touch

How you stay in touch and how often is up to you. If you have 50 clients, 500 clients, or 5,000 clients, the quantity will dictate what you can or cannot do. We use the holidays through the year. We also send birthday cards. When we started we bought blank cards by the box and wrote a note in each one. Now we design a unique birthday card for the year and every week we pull the labels from our database for the coming week and mail them.

You can also track your client's house anniversary date and mail a card that says Happy Second Year in your home. Many super agents use tax time to send a copy of last year's closing statement. The options are endless. Choose what works for you and keep in touch with your clients.

Another idea is the client appreciation party. Although we have never done this we know super agents who swear by them. How you get together can range from taking all your clients to a baseball game to getting together for a barbeque in your backyard. Your local cinema can schedule a private showing of a new movie. The possibilities are only limited by your imagination.

Because of the size of our past-client database, we now do contests. This gives us an opportunity to give a significant prize. We send instructions in the form of an insert with our greeting card and then send our clients to our website for details. Here's an example.

For Fourth of July we sent a patriotic greeting card and on vellum paper we announced a recipe contest. The prize was to be a big red Kitchen Aid mixer that it seems everyone covets. This contest was so popular we ended up giving away four mixers and our team appreciated the opportunity to judge entries for a month. This was three years ago and people still talk about the big red mixers today.

There are agents who ascribe to the practice of rating clients as *A*'s, *B*'s, or *C*'s. This may work fine but we have never done this. We find it difficult to predict which client will bring us more business than another so we treat them all the same.

We settled this after year two of our business. One day, ever the economizer, I asked JoAnn why we would bother to mail to our out-of-state past clients. We had sold their house and they had moved away. They were gone I reasoned. It was a waste of money. JoAnn said no and pulled out a current escrow file asking me if I knew where this client came from. Well, of course I knew. They were related somehow to the folks who moved to Missouri a few months before. But I played dumb, so she pulled out another example and another and I said okay, forget about it. Since that time, JoAnn has had the gleeful pleasure of telling me on a regular basis about this client or that client who sent us business from out of state.

Out-of-state clients still have family and friends back here. They know people where they are who plan to move to Arizona. And then, of course, they end up moving back. They say the road runs twice and you can believe it. People move from Scottsdale to North Scottsdale and in a few years they move back. It is the darnedest thing. I have no explanation for it, but I know it exists.

What about out of the country? Do you have any idea what it costs to mail a Christmas ornament to Perth, Australia? I do and I once again raised the issue with JoAnn around 2003. JoAnn of course prevailed and I want to expand here upon my confession of stupidity.

We had these nice clients call us to list their middle-class, 1980s, two-story suburban home nearby. There was nothing special about their home or them other than his charming accent. They moved to Perth. Now Perth is not even close to the United States. When you get to Sydney, you still have another 3,000 miles to go. Perth is on the west side of Australia. Perth is closer to Hong Kong than most of its neighbors. That year we mailed them their ornament. In the spring she called to ask us to sell their rental that they had left behind, thinking they could manage it from halfway around the world. We sold that and then she called to say they wanted to sell the ranch. What ranch, I thought. It was ten acres in North Scottsdale and had boarding facilities for 97 horses. It also had several arenas and turnouts and stuff we knew nothing about. We told her on the phone we had never handled anything like that and she said she would have no other agent, so we faxed the paperwork.

When we sold that ranch it was the largest sale we had ever made up to that time and in the years since, we have served the husband's friend and the wife's sister and several others. Today, I never question the expense of keeping in touch with past clients. It is the best money we spend and we look for ways to do more.

Past clients are your most basic lead source of all. If you never do any other type of lead generation, your past clients will feed you, keep you, and pay you the rest of your life.

Chapter 9 Summary

Better than Social Security

- Real estate is a repeat business.
- Past-client referrals are the best business.
- All it takes is 5 percent per year.

Build a Database

- Collect all the information you can.
- Select software.
- Software is only as good as you make it.

Return on Investment

- We send personalized Christmas ornaments.
- At a minimum, $300 gets you $6,000.
- Make an investment.

The Early Days

- Cookies and scoops.
- It's not about real estate—treat clients like family.
- Personalize it.

Sentiments

- Be sincere.
- It's okay to be silly.
- Write it yourself.

Closing Gifts

- Go beyond just the client.
- Set a regular schedule.
- Don't skimp.

Stay in Touch

- Year-round opportunities.
- Client parties.
- Contests.
- *A*, *B*, and C clients.
- Out-of-state clients.
- Out-of-country clients.
- Look for ways to touch clients.
- The best money you will ever spend.
- Past clients will keep you the rest of your life.

Super Lead Generation

"Give them quality. That's the best kind of advertising in the world."
—Milton Hershey, founder, the Hershey Chocolate Company

"Early to bed, early to rise, work like hell, and advertise."
—Ted Turner, founder, CNN

"All lead generation can be divided into two categories—prospecting and marketing."
—Chapter 10, page 96, *Super Agent*

10

A Steady Stream of Buyers and Sellers

Up to now we have only discussed the elementary things you, as a potential super agent, can and should do. First, be a good agent. Develop your super powers. Take care of your clients and keep in touch with your past clients because they are your most basic source of new business.

There comes a time, however, when past clients are just not enough. If you want to grow your business, if you want to go to whatever the next level is, you will need new business. Past clients are wonderful, you can have a nice career from them, and you can even retire with them but you cannot put them on a schedule. One month you might get several recommendation calls and the next you might receive none. You cannot force referrals.

When JoAnn and I began our real estate careers, we had no circle of influence. We spent every waking moment together. My only outside interest was JoAnn. Her only hobby was trying to fix me. Not that we were antisocial, we were just not out there like we are today.

Referrals and Recommendations

We were broke and needed the business. I remember saying to JoAnn, "Don't you think we should ask our clients for referrals?" and she replied she wasn't comfortable with that. It somehow went against her feelings of what was proper and so we just did the very best job we could and hoped those clients would bring their family and friends. Fortunately, because of our commitment to putting the client first, new business was attracted to us and unasked-for recommendations accounted for part of our growth.

It's not like I just gave up on the asking-for-referrals idea. Every six months or so, I would try again, and JoAnn would say no. My greatest victory on the referral front was the day I came up with "Thank you for all your kind words." The idea came from the old Bartles & Jaymes commercial where at the end of the 30 seconds, one of the two older gentlemen, who were the beverage maker's spokespersons, would say thank you again for all your support. So I came up with this kind-words phrase as a tagline to put on everything we sent out. It sort of assumed people were recommending us and I reasoned that if someone were not saying good things about us, this line might make them feel that others were and they would want to get on the bandwagon. Anyway, we put that line on most of the stuff we produce and I get to feel victorious. If you are shy about asking for referrals, feel free to use this phrase or something like it.

But referrals and recommendations do not grow a business, at least not at a spectacular rate, and that was what happened to us. Our business exploded.

Marta's Mission

Our very first assistant was Marta. We hired her to be the transaction coordinator and take clients through escrow. Most of our business was buyer deals from holding open houses. Our listings seemed to come from neighbors of the open houses and our SOLD riders that we hung under our yard sign as soon as we got into escrow. Marta cried over the first escrow repair request and we found our second assistant to do the job that Marta had no aptitude for. Marta was so creative and organized, however, that we couldn't let her go, so we made her our marketing person. I remember telling her that her mission was to create a steady stream of buyers and sellers.

We had bills to pay and no amount of business was enough, so we went after it with a great deal of vigor. We didn't have a fancy name for our efforts back then. We didn't call it lead generation. We only knew we needed a steady stream of buyers and sellers. We had no idea that much of what we were already doing was a form of lead generation. We just needed the business and forged ahead not knowing what it was that we were doing.

The first thing we did was to start advertising every week in our major newspaper, the *Arizona Republic*. We reasoned that our sellers had entrusted us to sell their homes and we should advertise them. Then we started mailing the one thousand homes around our house. We sent them Valentines in February and birthday cards in May because it was JoAnn's birthday. We had a gentleman named Arnold who came by with novelty items and we bought a thousand of this and a thousand of that and Marta kept track of it all. We held open houses regularly and gave out chip clips with our name on them. We bought pens with our name and used them at every signing. We called them lucky pens and the clients kept them. We had no idea this was lead generation but we did know it cost money.

Investing in Yourself

There are so many agents out there who just will not spend money on their business. There are also agents who waste money on their business because they don't understand lead generation and do not know what to do and when to do it. We will come to that, but for now we want to talk about agents who won't spend a dime. You cannot expect to grow your business, to build something lasting, without investing in yourself and your business.

The reason JoAnn and I were halfway through life and broke when we started in real estate is because we had just spent several years following our passion—books. We were book collectors, which is a nice way of saying we were book scouts. Actually, it started as yard sales with a specialty. Every weekend, we went to every sale we could, searching for collectable first editions. It was exciting and a thrill when we found Truman Capote's *In Cold Blood* for a dollar or Jaqueline Michard's *Deep End of the Ocean* that actually ended up in the bargain-book bin in local bookstores before her career took off and the book became rare. It was a treasure hunt and we loved it but we went broke because there were so many books we just couldn't part with. It was like the cookie maker eating the profits. By the time we got our real estate licenses we had over 10,000 books in our garage. They were the only asset we owned.

That first year in real estate, we sold our treasured books to pay for our real estate marketing. We were making commissions but they weren't enough. We had my dad to pay back, and living expenses, and a couple of assistants who we shared our commissions with and it took more money to cover it all, so we sold a few hundred of our books at a time to dealers we knew. We tell you this because investing in your future is just that important. When we sold my Clive Cusslers and JoAnn's Diane Gabaldons it was like parting with a piece of ourselves. We invested in making our business grow and it did. You must, too.

A Plan and a Budget

Now let's talk about overspending. If you don't have a plan and a budget, you can give back all you earn and have nothing to show for it. We see this all the time. We kept very careful track of how much was coming in and therefore, how much we could spend. We do this to this very day. You cannot just throw money at something and think it will get you results. You must budget and you must measure results. If you are not a numbers person, hire someone who is.

One of the reasons agents overspend is that they have no idea what to spend it on because they have no idea what lead generation is in the first place. They just hear that they need to be generating leads and they buy into the first thing that comes along. You must learn what lead generation is and then you must decide how you wish to pursue it. You need a plan.

JoAnn and I do it this way. She decides what she wants us to do and I figure out how to afford it. As a general rule, we spend 10 percent of our gross-commission income on lead generation. Rules, however, are made to be broken and when it comes to breaking the rules about money, I cannot remember when that meant spending less. There are times when it makes sense to spend more. McDonalds spends a small percentage of their income on advertising. They spend it every day, every week. They have a plan and they stick to it. But a part of that plan allows for opening new locations and when they do that, they budget extra to promote the new restaurant. We figure if it's good enough for Mickey D, then it's good enough for us.

When our business seemed to be doing pretty well, we decided to expand our mailings from 1,000 to 3,000 homes. Our volume at that point wasn't enough to do this and stay within our 10 percent budget so we made the decision to spend more in order to expand. We've done this many times and today we mail to over 30,000 homes but we never exceeded 20 percent of our income. We know this because we track the numbers and so should you.

Consistency

We've had our share of flops. Some of the best ideas on paper seem to fizzle in practice and when they do we have given them up. If the horse you are riding is dead, get off. As a quick aside, I have to tell you that imitation is the greatest form of flattery and we have been copied many times. The cute thing about this is that the imitators invariably pick our disappointments, the genius failures, to emulate and when we see it we roll with laughter. Anyway, not everything succeeds and some things succeed at different rates than others. When you do find something that works for you, stick with it. There are just not enough winners out there for you to jump off a horse that is getting you there just because another one is pretty. Consistency will trump genius almost every time. We can't all be geniuses, but we can all be consistent.

Just when you think you can't look at another ad or newsletter, that's when your audience is beginning to notice. We have mailed the same postcard for more than 10 years and it works. Oh we've tried others to mixed reviews but this one works and we stay with it. We get clients who have only seen this piece briefly for years as they tossed it in the trash and then the weekend they decide to sell, they see it, and it clicks because they remember all those times they threw it away. You don't have to be a whiz. All you have to do is find a few things that work and be consistent.

Lead Generation

As we said, we had no idea what we were doing. We only knew we had to spend a portion of our income back into our growth and we tried everything we could. If only we had known what lead generation was, we could have saved so much time and money. This seems to be a pervasive disconnect in our industry because we speak often to groups and when it comes to the question-and-answer part of the hour, the first question is, "What should I do next or how should I generate leads?"

Agents just don't understand. We didn't. They try this and try that and hope to get lucky. Well, that is just too risky. You need to understand lead generation. You need to know what you are doing, why you are doing it, and how to do it. When you do, your business will be transformed and you too will be a super agent.

All lead generation can be divided into two categories—prospecting and marketing.

When you are prospecting, you are proactively going after the customer. Examples of prospecting are cold calling on the phone or in person, warm calling in person or on the phone, striking up a real estate conversation everywhere you go and handing out your business card, soliciting for sale by owners (FSBOs), soliciting expired listings, networking, and so on. The action here is that you are going after the business.

When you are marketing, you are attracting the customer to come to you. You are making the phone ring. Examples of marketing are advertising in print, on media, and through direct mail, branding, publicity, signage, and so forth. The action here is that you are making the business come to you.

That's it—only two methods. Not complicated, but people try to make it complex and mysterious all the time. You create a steady stream of buyers and sellers both by going out and getting them and by getting them to come to you.

Evolution and You

Early humans survived on their wits. All that they had, they went out and found. They found a cave for shelter. They found wood for fire. They found nuts and berries and they hunted animals to eat. Paleontologists called early humans *hunter-gatherers*. Their very existence was tested every day. Every day they had to find food or die. Many found they had to keep moving as plant supplies and available game were used up. Hunter-gatherers were nomadic.

At some point somebody discovered that they could plant and nurture nut trees and berry bushes and any number of other fruits, grains, and vegetables. Suddenly they didn't have to move on. They could put down roots along with their crops. Villages grew into cities and these planter-growers brought their bounty to sell and markets were born. That's where the word *marketing* comes from.

Agents who generate leads by prospecting are hunter-gatherers and agents who generate leads by marketing are planter-growers. Both methods are valid. Hunting and gathering still sustains a large portion of the world's population and, of course, the rest of us are fed from restaurants and supermarkets.

Whichever method you choose, and you may choose a mix from both options, you need to understand what it is you are doing when you are doing it. We believe it is in not understanding what we are doing that the confusion lies. Just as shooting somebody else's cow is not hunting, you won't be successful trying to herd mountain lions for Burger King to sell cougar burgers.

Mindset

As a super agent, you know your success is up to you. Whether or not your stream of buyers and sellers exists, how big it is, how fast it flows, and the quality of those leads is up to you. You are in control of your own destiny. As master of your fate you have the power to manage your expectations. You don't have to live up to anyone else's expectations, just yours. When it comes to lead generation you must know what you are doing in order to manage your expectations A super agent always knows what they are doing and why. You are either prospecting or marketing. Understanding when you are doing one or the other can make a huge difference in how you plan and prepare. If you approach marketing with a prospecting mindset, you will be quickly disappointed and abandon your plan long before it can yield results. If you approach prospecting with a marketing mindset you will fail to act swiftly when the opportunity presents itself.

It's Up to You

You can decide for yourself what your business looks like and how much business you have or you can leave it to chance and let the market decide for you. Most agents don't want to decide. They want to leave it up to their broker and when their broker is exhausted with trying to help them help themselves, they switch brokers thinking the grass is somehow always greener next door. Don't be that agent. Don't be average. You want to be a super agent and the good news is that everything, all the success and satisfaction and rewards, is right there in your heart. You get to decide.

Do you remember the three characteristics of a super agent in Chapter 1? We call them the three *D*'s and they are decision, drive, and determination. If you are to build your business and grow your numbers, you will need all three of these and the first is decision. You must decide where you want your business to go. You can stay where you are, move forward, or quit and find another vocation. It is up to you. If your decision is to grow, then lead generation is your vehicle to get you there.

Our business today is changing because the market is changing and we learned early on that you cannot ignore the market and expect it to comply with the way you like to do things. We mirror the market. We have stayed current as we went from faxes to e-mails to text messaging. But some things have not changed. Our basic principals of putting the client first, honesty, competence, and care, have not waivered even once. And our commitment to lead generation has been constant.

Only Your Time

There is another option and you may wish to choose it. JoAnn and I did this in a way. We put money back into our business, which wasn't easy because of the bills, and we also invested a lot of our time. This is the other option. You can spend every free moment you have on lead generation methods that cost only your time.

This method can be very rewarding. We know many agents who swear by this and achieve success. The only problem is that there is a limited supply of time while somewhere out there is an unlimited supply of money. You may buy time—we will discuss that later—but money is much more direct. By the time we were three years in real estate we were working over 100 hours a week. We don't do that anymore. We invest money into making money and that is better for us.

Selling real estate is just this simple; *unless you are with a client, or doing something for a client, you should be generating leads.* That's it. Build your business by getting more. Control your destiny by generating leads. The trick is to know how to lead generate. When you know how, you will always know what to do next.

Chapter 10 Summary

If You Want to Grow Your Business You Need New Business

- Past clients are not enough.
- You cannot force referrals.
- If you can't ask, thank them for all their kind words.

Marta's Mission

- A steady stream of buyers and sellers.
- Forge ahead.
- Keep track of it all.

Invest in Yourself

- Spend but don't overspend.
- Have a plan.
- Have a budget.

Consistency

- People copy cute.
- Consistency trumps genius.
- Just when you are sick of it, people start to notice.

Lead Generation

- Prospecting or marketing.
- Hunter-gatherers.
- Planter-growers.

Mindset

- Manage your expectations.
- It's all up to you.
- You get to decide.

Your Time

- If you have no money, invest your time.
- Always be generating leads.
- Always know what to do next.

11 Prospecting

Prospecting is at once the most exciting and the most maligned activity you may undertake. Prospecting can find you a new client before noon or it can freeze you with so much fear that you are still in bed well past lunchtime. To succeed at prospecting, we must focus on the excitement and find ways to alleviate the pain.

Our broker had a training program for new agents and we attended a few classes before we were invited to not come back. JoAnn and I can be a little rebellious and we tended to be in a hurry, so we didn't make the best students. It's something we regret today, but you can't go back. Our instructor, however, was a big fan of a national trainer who was coming to town and before exiting the classes we had signed up for this gentleman's two-day seminar.

Cold Calling

When the time for the event came, JoAnn and I disagreed over what to do. She had a lady she wanted to show houses to and I wanted to go to the seminar because we had already paid for the tickets. This reasoning is a personality flaw I readily admit to, along with cleaning my plate and not asking for directions. Our solution, which I deeply regret because I should have supported JoAnn, was to split up. I would go and JoAnn would show. As a result I spent more than a week in the doghouse and was introduced to the wonderful world of cold-call prospecting.

Remember, this was 1997. The No Call list did not exist. The seminar was attended by well over 500 agents who by the end of the two days were committed to spending three hours every morning making phone calls to perfect strangers, reciting scripts I had trouble reading, much less sounding sincere. I would venture to guess that the fervor wore off quickly and I doubt any of these agents were still working the phones two weeks later. I know I never tried but I did learn a lot about fear because this man and his crew were fearless. They would call anyone. They would say anything and they had no fear of the consequences. So great was their confidence, out of respect I must give them credit for some valuable wisdom.

Don't be afraid to lose what you don't have. It is such a simple statement and obviously correct but I found it astounding for I had been guilty of this all my life. Somehow, in those two days, I shed this fear just by hearing it phrased this way. You cannot lose what you do not have. You can fail to get something you want. But that is not the same thing. If you want something and do not ask for it, the chances of getting it are very close to nil. If you ask for it badly, you still may not get it but at least you tried. Pity the dying person whose regret is that they wish they had tried. Don't be afraid to lose what you don't have.

The gentleman on stage gave this wonderful example for handling rejection. He said that David Letterman, host of his long-running late night show on television, would at least once a week have a segment in which he read jokes off of index cards. Some worked and some bombed and when they stunk, David would flip the card over his shoulder into the backdrop. Our speaker said this was how to handle rejection. He told us to mentally flip the index card over our shoulder and to say *next* in our mind. I have never forgotten that image and it has served me well.

I learned a number of other things in those two days, some good, some bad, and most of all I learned to never go to a seminar alone again.

That image of prospecting stayed with me for years and I often said I would never prospect. What I didn't realize was that many of the things we did were a form of prospecting. We just did not know we were doing it.

Before going on we want to say that cold calling is still a valid prospecting method. Over the years JoAnn and I have attended, together, a number of events and heard a number of speakers espouse the virtues of working the phones every day. They may call it warm calling and give a list of targets but it is still the same thing. The challenge with this approach is that it is hard to maintain the pace and resolve over the long haul. Those who can, we salute you, but as super agents we know there are other ways.

Prospecting without Knowing

When we said we were prospecting without knowing it we meant that many of the things we did that came naturally and comfortably to us were in fact prospecting. Any time we were going out to get the clients we were prospecting.

An example of this is follow up. If someone were to suggest calling a prospect was the same thing as calling a stranger I would dispute it, but we call clients all the time seeking their business. When we show someone a house and then a couple of days later we follow up and call, we are prospecting. That's right, we are going after the business and that is prospecting.

When we hold an open house and greet them at the door we are prospecting. They may be there to see the home but we are there to pick them up as clients. In fact, if prospecting can be likened to hunting, then open house is like sitting in a duck blind with a caller at your lips waiting for a mallard to fly by.

Because you may not have thought of these activities as prospecting, you may be missing the most exciting experiences you can have. Think about all you do and you may be surprised to find you are already prospecting and don't know it.

Excitement

When Christmas comes we have a number of team members who want the 26th of December off because of the sales. These bargain hunters are up at midnight planning their day. They read the ads and arrive at each store at just the right moment. They are excited.

What excites you? I remember going fishing as a boy. I couldn't sleep the night before. Deer hunters can't wait for hunting season. Cyber Monday sets new sales records each year. People get car fever when they go shopping for a new car and, yes, folks get excited looking for a new home. These are all examples of prospecting, going after what you want, and they are all exciting.

Then why do agents spend their morning checking e-mail, visiting with other agents, and doing just about anything and everything but calling a client or planning an open house? It is all mindset. They have no understanding of what prospecting is and consequently they are not excited.

Opportunity

Prospecting is the opportunity to put yourself in a position to succeed right now, immediately, no waiting. Think about it. When you are showing a house or taking a call or otherwise engaging someone in a conversation about real estate, you are only seconds away from a client moving forward. A simple question from you may get a positive answer. This is prospecting and it is exciting.

Once you know when you are prospecting, you can plan your hunt. You can get excited. You can recognize your fear and deal with it. Bravery is not a condition of having no fear. Bravery is a matter of facing your fear and acting anyway. Be brave, be excited, and lay out your plan. Now you must decide on whom, how, and when to prospect.

Targeting

Who you pursue is the first element in your plan. So many agents don't have a clue about whom. This is one of the great things about prospecting—you get to pick whom to pursue, so you can specialize in a particular target group and become very insightful and competent at serving their needs. Also, if you tire of a certain group, you can take your prospecting skills elsewhere because you get better with practice. The only skill you need to prospect is the ability to be a super motivator and ask questions. And the more you ask, the better you get.

Here is a partial list of target groups to choose from. These are by no means all your choices. It seems we hear a new twist on this list daily. Here are the standards.

- **The phone book.** Not as easy as it used to be, but you never run out of people, and the skills you develop put you at the top of the heap.
- **Everyone you talk to.** Again, not for the faint of heart or shy, but you have an endless supply of targets. When you can walk into a shopping mall and come out with a client, you will never be hungry again.
- **Networking within a special-interest group.** This is within everybody's reach. Think church group, hobby group, and business group. We know an agent who found all her business within her PTA group. Our daughter is a quilter so we have many quilting clients. Sometimes just mentioning that you are an agent is enough, but

being a member of a group makes for easy conversation. Just make sure it is about real estate.

- **For sale by owners.** This is one of the most lucrative target groups because they have already announced their desire to sell. They have also announced a resistance to using an agent or paying a commission. This is also a very competitive arena. However, many of these competing agents come and go. The agent who sticks with this category and develops the right questions and responses can dominate.

- **Expired listings.** Like the FSBOs above, your target wants to sell but unlike the FSBO they want an agent. However, you must deal with their despair and skepticism. And you must compete with the hordes of other agents, who sometimes call before 6 a.m. the morning the computer announces the seller's new status. You may choose to compete early or you might choose to work the 30-day-old group. In most markets, about half of the expireds relist in the first 30 days, but the other half eventually return to the market up to six months later.

- **You can target life-changing events.** Every day, people get married, have children, retire, or pass away. These events often trigger a change of real estate. We know an agent in another state who works the public records for bankruptcies, foreclosure notices, marriage licenses, and so on. Another agent we know follows the business news and calls promoted executives to congratulate them.

- **Absentee owners.** Your title company can get you lists of people who don't live in the house. This makes them landlords and by contacting them you may find out they are tired of the job or they may be investors looking for a new agent—you.

- **Part-time residents.** Narrow the preceding list to out-of-state owners and you may get people who are starved for information on your local market.

The possibilities are endless and you get to choose. There should never be a moment in the career of a super agent when you don't know what to do next.

Methods

The next step in your prospecting plan is to decide your method. All prospecting is not conducted through direct communication. Prospecting is not done en masse. The minute you are communicating to more than one individual, you are marketing.

Face to face is your number one method of communication with another person. All your senses are engaged. You can use body language and judge theirs. You can hold their attention or at least know when you have lost it. The more time you spend face to face with clients and prospects the more your career will soar.

Telephone is your next choice of communication. It is amazing how many average agents resist picking up the phone to talk to clients. They find every excuse to put calls off. They look for alternatives, such as texting and e-mailing. Phone calls are opportunities knocking. We have fourteen lines coming into our office and sometimes they are all busy. Add to that all the cell phones and we are talking to a lot of people all day long.

Let me add a philosophical note here. It has been our experience that no situation has ever been made worse by talking to a client. If a meeting or a call exposes a problem then at least we have an opportunity to fix whatever it is. Prospecting is all about opportunity. Agents complain that they don't have opportunities and then they get a message and say, "I'll call them back later." They are squandering an opportunity because they don't know that prospecting is opportunity. They let the fear take away their chances and at the end of the day they wonder why they don't do better.

Lastly, you can prospect digitally or through the mail. Have you ever thought of a personal, handwritten note as prospecting? It is a one-on-one communication and it's an opportunity. It is prospecting and it is exciting. How much different the task is when you think of it as an opportunity to connect. We know an agent who resolved to write three handwritten notes a day for a year. Just three—but he didn't take weekends off and at the end of the year he had mailed almost 1,100 cards—and it doubled his business.

The beauty of prospecting is that when you know and understand it for what it is you will seek it rather than dread it. You will look for opportunity rather than shun it. The best part is you get to choose whom, how, and when. You can do this.

Chapter 11 Summary

Cold Calling

- Don't be afraid to lose what you don't have.
- Just say next.
- Hard to maintain the pace and resolve.

Prospecting Without Knowing

- Follow up is prospecting.
- Open house is prospecting.
- Think about other things you already do.

Excitement

- What excites you?
- Going after what you want.
- Understand what prospecting is.

Opportunity

- Prospecting puts you in a position to succeed immediately.
- Plan your hunt.
- Bravery is facing your fear.

Targeting—A Partial List

- The phone book.
- Everyone you talk to.
- Networking within a special interest group.
- For Sale By Owner.
- Expired listings.
- Life-changing events.
- Absentee owners.
- Part-time residents.

Methods

- Face to face.
- Telephone.
- Digitally or through the mail.

12 Open Houses

Open house is the ultimate form of prospecting, and most agents don't even know it. It's like shopping online: there's no need to traipse from one store to the next because they come to you. It's true that an open house is a form of marketing since clients come to you but the interaction is all one on one, so you are truly prospecting. It can be reasoned that an open house is a hybrid or marriage of both prospecting and marketing. An open house is so lucrative it's a wonder that some agents question its value.

As we travel the country and speak to agents, we get the question, "Do you hold open houses?" It seems to come with the implied question, "Which side are you on?" as if there were two warring camps, for and against open houses. You need to understand both points of view so that you may guide your seller to a successful sale.

A Bad Idea

At listings we have had potential sellers ask about open house. More often than not they want to make sure we will open their home. But occasionally they ask because the previous agent (yes, some sellers interview more than one agent) sold them on the idea that open houses are a waste of time. You may have had this same experience or you may even be one of those agents promoting this point of view.

As we understand it the explanation goes something like this. Open houses are a bad idea. Statistics show there is a better chance of snow in July than having a contract written at an open house. The only people who come are nosy neighbors. It is a security risk. Burglars use open houses to case their next robbery. Female agents are at risk and you don't want *that* happening in your home. Agents just use your home to pick up buyers and take them to other homes for sale. The implication here is that they will sell your competitor's home before they sell yours. I'm sure the list goes on and on. Open-house bashing is a fairly easy target. Why do these agents take this approach? I do not know if they believe every word or if they just don't want to do open houses. What I do know is that they are missing a huge opportunity to build their business.

It Does Snow in July

At Those Callaways, we hold open houses every Friday, Saturday, and Sunday, and here are just a few of the reasons.

An open house sells our seller's home. Apparently it does snow in July because we have written contracts at the open house. In fact, one time we had three agents writing in three different rooms as they haggled back and forth. The winner removed all contingencies and closed in a week.

We get calls on Monday, Tuesday, and Wednesday from agents who need to preview our listing because their clients were playing hooky on the weekend and want their agent to see the house now. We get offers that come in without a record of a showing only to find out that this agent's clients saw the house weeks or even months ago at an open house.

Yes, we do pick up buyers and they often do not buy the home we are holding open. However, and we point this out to all our sellers, the fact that we are holding open houses means that while we may not be holding yours open, we may very well be finding your buyer at another home that we are holding open.

Every week the buyer pool changes. Some find a home, some keep looking, and some new buyers enter the hunt. Because we are out there every week we have an opportunity to keep our finger on the pulse of the market. As homes come on the market we have a list of people to call. As homes sell, we know who got one and who didn't. This market knowledge is part of the value package we bring to our clients.

We get listings from those neighbors who come see the house. That is, after all, a good reason for a neighbor to come by. And to think that nosy neighbors are one of the negatives quoted by the agent who doesn't believe in open houses. We get listings because we say, "Yes, we do open houses," at the listing presentation instead of trying to dissuade sellers from the idea.

You may have to sell the idea of an open house to your seller if a naysayer has gotten to your client first. Be ready to expand on all these benefits of holding an open house with your client. It will pay them big dividends.

A Wonderful Opportunity

We've talked about some of the obvious seller advantages of open house, but what's in it for you, the agent? Just imagine, the buyers have already qualified themselves on so many levels. They've identified the area as a place they would like to live. They parked the car so they like the architecture. It's likely that they know about the schools and shopping. They may not know the price but it's probably in their range. You don't even need to build a store or stock the shelves. What a wonderful opportunity to connect in a great setting.

Additionally, you have the opportunity to put your signs on the street. People see your name. Even if they are not moving now, they will think of you when they are ready. Every night, someone out there decides to move. You want your name to be the one they think of when this happens.

Ads work better (way better) when you are advertising an event and what better event than an open house? We run call-to-see ads and the phone doesn't ring. We hold an open house and get from 50 to 250 people in a three-hour period.

Our open-house advertising gets us List Me calls. Think about it. You decide to sell, what do you do? You look in the paper or online to see who is selling property.

Speaking of online, we get more hits on the open-house section of our website than any other part.

Preparation

Once you've decided to hold an open house, remember to go big or go home. We call it mega-open-house and it takes preparation. We don't decide the last thing on Friday and hold an open home on Saturday. A good idea planned ahead beats a great last-minute idea every time. We work at least a week or two ahead. We have a roster. We put them on the website on Monday. We schedule which agent is going to hold the open house and they prepare by searching the MLS and understanding every home on the market. We hang riders saying "Open Saturday." We think ahead and make it timely like giving a rose to each lady on Mother's Day. When it is a big listing and the crowd expectation is high we have more than one agent hosting. One agent at a busy open house ends up doing traffic control rather than relationship building and engagement. We have handouts and giveaways. We prepare and that makes all the difference.

What You Need to Know

Preparation is everything. One of the three keys to put the client first is competence and the secret to competence is preparation. We take our classes in preparation to pass the state exam. Then we must learn all that we can to practice our profession with competence.

Several years ago Martha Stewart, who is a good friend of Donald Trump, did a one-season spinoff of Donald's highly successful *Apprentice* television show. It was all done with Donald's blessing and closely followed the Trump formula except that the firing process was one of Martha sending a handwritten note to the contestant who would not be continuing. This was very proper, as only Martha Stewart can be. Well, one of the favorites on the show was a tall blonde young lady with potential written all over her and she survived through the first several episodes. Then she made her fatal mistake. While working on a project and in earshot of Martha, she innocently repeated a phrase we hear all the time, "you have to fake it 'til you make it." As you might imagine, the turkey droppings hit the windmill and all of America was treated to the Martha Stewart look. "What did you say?" Martha asked, wanting to be sure she had heard correctly. This is where my memory fails as I was whooping and laughing at my television too hard to remember Martha's exact words, but needless to say, the blonde girl got a not-so-nice note at the end of the show.

I'm sure I was guilty of saying those innocent words myself in the past. But the truth of putting clients first and being honest means you just cannot take people's trust and fake it till you make it. You must get competent and your first step can be getting ready for open house.

Know the House

Donna has done almost 3,000 open houses for us over the years and she always asks on Monday if I know which homes she is sitting next weekend. She asks because she wants to prepare. As soon as she knows which homes, she pulls the listing files to learn everything she can. She examines the notes for little things like gate codes, security codes, the children's names, the pet's names, where the switch is to the fountain, why there is a step in an odd place, what additions were constructed and when? She studies the MLS and learns how much the homeowner's association fee is, what it covers, how much are the taxes, the utilities, and any other small pieces of information she must know. She looks at tax records, if there is a recent appraisal, were they listed before, what is the pricing history? Donna wants to know all she can about our seller's and their situation so she won't get blindsided at the open house. If it is a new listing or one she has not seen before, she makes an appointment to preview the home. When she enters she looks at the home with buyer's eyes. She asks herself what will a buyer want to know and then she makes sure she has the answers. This is preparation.

Know the Neighborhood

Donna doesn't stop there. She often already knows the neighborhood but occasionally the home is in a new area for her or an area she hasn't been to in a while. She makes it her business to know the schools, including the bus routes, the hours, the holidays and vacation schedules, whether it is open enrollment or closed, and a hundred other details. Donna knows the drive times, when the trash truck comes, where to shop, where to eat, what the HOA allows and doesn't allow. She knows the parks, all the plusses and yes, all the negatives so she can address any potential buyer's concerns. This is preparation.

Know the Competition

At her computer, Donna pulls more than just the MLS. She searches all the active listings in the area. She looks at their stats and photos and, if needed, she will do a drive-by or even preview homes most like our listing. Donna will print out the competition's listings and is ready to show them after the open house if she picks up a client who doesn't care for the home she is sitting. Also, Donna will look at what is in escrow and what has sold recently. She knows that buyers will ask about this information and she wants to be prepared to answer their questions with confidence. When Donna goes to put out her signs, she is ready. She gets there at least 15 minutes early and she knows the house, the neighborhood, and the competition.

I'm Here. Now What?

I've walked into open houses where it looks like the agent has packed for summer camp. They have their laptop or iPad, usually set up for Angry Birds or Solitaire. They have their brown bag lunch or worse yet, they went through a drive-through on the way and now the house smells of French fries. Some have a book, usually a paperback, a good beach read. They usually say nothing or a simple hello from the kitchen and when you get through seeing the home they point to the open house register laying open on the countertop and they say something about the seller wanting you to register your visit. At other open houses I've visited, the agent seems prepared but they spend the whole time on the phone. They are catching up on callbacks, or placing prospect calls, or worse yet, they are trying to deal with a dissatisfied client. This is usually done in such a loud voice you can hear them from the master bath. In all these examples the expectation seems to be that the open house represents time to be passed rather than the magnificent opportunity it is. Why do they bother? The most common answer given is that they do it to satisfy the unreasonable seller who wants an open house. Probably the real answer is that they just don't know what to do or say.

Showing the Home

Let's start at the front door. I even know a very successful agent who starts outside on the porch. His explanation to me was that if they didn't want to give him their information, he didn't want them walking around the house. While it may work for him, we recommend the foyer as the best place to greet visitors. JoAnn, on the other hand, likes to wait in the kitchen with her legal pad while she appears to be making notes, an easily interruptible activity. Here is where we realize that everyone is an individual and how you handle the greeting is personal to you. The important thing is that you greet visitors and make them feel welcome. Your goal is to make a connection, establish a relationship, and you cannot expect strangers to work very hard at seeking you out. Yes, you might wait for a question, but remember the person asking the questions is the one in control. Once greeted, it is important to give visitors some latitude to look at the home. Some agents prefer to walk people around pointing out features and benefits. While this may work for some agents and for some potential clients it is best to make them feel free to look. It is, after all, an *open* house not a tour house. Also, it has been our experience that folks are more guarded when they first enter a strange home. The longer they look, the more relaxed they become.

Picking Up Clients

Wouldn't it be great if you could just have a three-question card that everyone filled out and handed to you as they came in? It would ask: Are you working with another agent? Are you ready and able to buy now? How much do you want to spend? Sitting open houses would be like shooting fish in a barrel. Unfortunately it isn't that easy, so we need to get those answers in other ways. This is called qualifying.

Let's talk about question number one. Are they working with another agent? The reality is that visitors are often playing hooky from their agent who is out of town, with another client at that moment, or even scheduled to meet them at another house and they saw your signs on the way. Certainly it is your responsibility to your seller to market their home but it is also your ethical responsibility to respect another agent's agency relationship. Some agents want to cut a fine line here. They ask questions like—Have you signed something with that other agent? They might even try to schedule showing this other agent's client a home that the open-house agent describes as a pocket listing or as just what you are looking for. Don't do it. Always err on the side of caution.

There are too many potential buyers out there without resorting to stealing from another agent. Ours is a small world and such efforts will come home to roost. Instead, ask questions: Have you looked at a lot of homes? Have you been looking for a while? How does this compare to what you've seen? These questions open people up and as they do so they will tell you if there is another agent. If, after this initial opening up and only after you've established a connection, they do not mention another agent and you are still not sure, then ask them straight out. This is an answer you must know.

Question two is: Are you ready and able to buy now? You need to know this. If they are months away from buying, you may want to capture their information and incubate the lead rather than show them three homes and then find out their timetable is long range. If they have not qualified with a lender or they are unable to do so, you need to know. As with question one, there are many questions that can lead to the answer you need. Questions such as these will lead them in the right direction: Is your current home sold? Do you already have a lender? Again, if you still don't know after establishing some rapport, then ask them directly.

Question three—How much can you or do you want to spend?—is the first step in getting their criteria. You must get this right or you risk the client saying to a future agent, "They (meaning you) didn't show me anything I wanted." Here is where the Internet is such a blessing. Simply ask if they have looked at homes online and at the right moment ask what price range they entered. Or, you might just ask how this house, the one you're sitting, compares in price to others they've seen. Again, you must ask questions but first you must begin a relationship.

Keep It Honest

Do not lie. Don't fudge. Don't evade questions. Keep it honest! Open house is fraught with temptation and you must resist. You will sleep better and people will be drawn to your forthrightness. You may never know when it happens, but some people will test you by asking questions to which they already know the answer. Demure or give them misinformation and you are doomed. Remember, we discussed competence. You must know the house, know the neighborhood, and know the competition. The more you know the more accurate you become. Seek the truth. Trust the truth and you will pick up more clients than you can handle.

Urgency

At the first open house we sat JoAnn diligently got prospects' names and phone numbers and then, because it wasn't proper to be pushy, JoAnn waited a week to call. This was 1997 in a so-so market with interest rates at 8 percent; when she called all but one potential client had found a house or were now working with another agent. Lesson learned. When people want a house, they want a house now. Once engaged you must stay engaged and here is where urgency can be your friend. One way to do this is to dangle the carrot. Offer to run a search and e-mail or deliver it. If you have a listing coming soon that they might like, tell them. Remember to keep it honest but brainstorm your personal situation and find ways to add urgency. If they like the home you are sitting and you have been busy with lots of traffic, tell them so. That's an opportunity to build urgency. Ask if you can show them another house right after the open house. After all, they are already in the neighborhood and you already pulled all those competitive listing. Do it now. Get their phone numbers. Get their e-mail. Get their criteria. Get their permission and follow up right away. Use their urgency as your friend and build a relationship right now.

Your goal at an open house is to pick up clients. Yes, you want to sell the home you are sitting and this does happen. But you also serve your seller by picking up clients at every open house. Your seller doesn't care if their buyer came from their open house or from holding an open a house ten blocks away. Your seller just wants a buyer and you want more clients.

Open houses will always be your number one opportunity to connect with ready buyers. Get excited the night before. Be prepared. Hold an open house today and write an offer before the sun goes down. You can do this.

Chapter 12 Summary

Not everyone recommends holding an open house.

A Bad Idea

- Only neighbors.
- Security risk.
- Agents just use open houses to pick up clients to whom they sell other homes.

It Does Snow in July

- We do sell homes at the open house.
- Neighbors have family or friends who buy and they also list.
- Every week the buyer pool changes.

(continued)

(*continued*)

A Wonderful Opportunity

- Buyers have already prequalified themselves as to price, neighborhood, and visual appeal.
- Signs on the street with your name.
- Ads work best for an event.

Preparation

- Go big or go home.
- Plan ahead.
- Do your research.

What You Need to Know

- Know the house.
- Know the neighborhood.
- Know the competition.

I'm Here, Now What?

- Don't be hard to interrupt.
- Greet in the foyer.
- Make a connection.

Picking Up Clients

- Are you working with another agent?
- Are you ready and able to buy now?
- How much do you want to spend?

Keep It Honest

- Do not evade questions.
- Respect agency.
- Trust the truth.

Urgency

- Find reasons for them to buy now.

13 Marketing

As exciting as prospecting is, there is a limit on how many prospects you can be in front of in a day. A face-to-face meeting is both the best method and the most limiting due to time constraints. JoAnn's day may seem like one long phone call but she still doesn't talk to more than a hundred people before the clock closes her down. Welcome to marketing where the sky is the limit.

Through marketing you can reach thousands, even tens of thousands, of people at one moment. Through marketing you can dominate in days. Your only limitation is money and, as we know, the money ultimately comes from results, and results come from effectiveness, so effective marketing is the key that unlocks the treasure-house door.

Only Two Things to Decide

Effective marketing makes the phone ring. Effective marketing turns you into the pursued instead of the pursuer. Super agents who last are effective marketers. What you do once that phone rings is vital and we will discuss that, but first you have decisions to make.

There are only two things to decide in marketing and that is the medium and the message. Everything else you do serves you in making those decisions and remaking them every day. That's right, marketing is a moving target. You cannot just layout your marketing for the year and walk away. You cannot hand over the promotion of your business and not be involved in the measurement of the results. Agents do this daily. They buy a postcard promotion and a month later, after they've been busy with clients, offers, and closings, they have no idea how that postcard impacted their business.

Stay Connected

Remember, super agents are super accountable. They run their practice as a business. They plan and they budget and they measure results. You must stay connected to that which brings you success.

An agent we know is a Scientologist and he makes this connection point by example using one of the best-known Scientologists of all. He tells us that John Travolta made the mistake of disconnecting. John was and is a super talent. When John Travolta made *Saturday Night Fever*, the entire country went into a disco frenzy. When he did *Urban Cowboy* we all shed our polyester for denim and learned the two-step. So great was John's influence on popular culture that he would make a movie and we would all go crazy. Then John stopped. He decided to raise kids and fly planes; it may have been the best of decisions for his life at the time but he disconnected from that which gave him success and after some years he could not get a good movie. Our friend goes on to say that when John Travolta read the script for *Pulp Fiction* he wanted the part so much he agreed to do the movie for next to nothing. He knew this was the vehicle to reconnect and it was.

I have to tell you, we took our grandchildren to see *Pulp Fiction* the first week it came out. JoAnn loves John Travolta and we had no idea what it was about. Our grandchildren were around 10, 9, and 8. We left less than 10 minutes into the film because of the profanity and violence. I have yet to see the whole thing from start to finish. I catch bits and pieces on television before I have to change channels but it restarted John Travolta's career and he has not disconnected since.

People used to say that Madonna was such a good businessperson as if it were a surprise, because we used to think that business came naturally to men and Madonna was an exception. Since that time we've seen interviews with Beyonce, Taylor Swift, and Lady Gaga, in which they all talk about how connected they are to the details of their marketing. These women know that only they can decide who they are and what the public's perception should be.

Are we comparing super agents to superstars? Why not? Within your market you can be as big as you decide you want your marketing to be.

The Mediums

You have to choose the medium that works for you. You must be comfortable. It is your marketing and you must decide. Here is an overview of the choices with a few pros and cons.

- **Direct mail**. It dawned on us a while back that while buyers are out searching for a home, sellers are in the home they want to sell. The most direct connection to these homeowners is the U.S. mail. We get asked about first-class postage versus bulk and here is the difference. With first class you get the undeliverable pieces back, so you can clean your list. Unless you want to spend a lot of money you have a one-ounce limit. With bulk mail you don't get the undeliverables returned but you do get a huge discount, and you can go up to 3.5 ounces, enough for a small magazine or tabloid-size newspaper. Every-door direct is a popular version of bulk mailing; since you do not have to put an addressee on your piece there is more space for your message. Check with the postal service for the rules. In spite of the expense, direct mail is your quickest path to sellers and getting a listing can justify a lot of direct mail.

- **Print advertising**. Any printed piece, whether it is a property flyer, a personal brochure, a daily, weekly, monthly, or a quarterly publication, is simply called print. With print your options are huge. Paper choices alone can run the gambit from newsprint to glossy, from card stock to thin, and everything in between. With print the piece has a long shelf life. People keep printed advertising. They file it away for a rainy day. They touch it and feel it and connect with you through the paper it is printed on. Print should always be a part of your image.

- **Signage and outdoor advertising**. The advantage with signage is you can control it daily. You can change the message quickly and signage works for you 24/7. Signs on the street can give you instant credibility. After all, people reason, if those people chose you to sell their house, you must be qualified. In real estate the yard sign is your most powerful marketing tool; when you hang a SOLD rider below it, the phone rings with list-me calls.

- **Broadcast**. Radio, television, and cable can be very effective for a real estate agent. The cost per thousand is low but the waste can be excessive. Unless you are willing to go wherever the message goes, many who hear your message won't care. Also, you are only making an impression. The only thing your recipient has is the memory of that impression. If you serve a large area and have a unique message, broadcast may be your medium.

- **Events.** You can market yourself to large groups in the form of seminars or broker opens. This is almost a hybrid of prospecting, since you are connecting face to face but not directly to one individual. If you are a good speaker this can be an excellent path.
- **Publicity.** Put the members of the press to work for you. If you are good at finding an interesting story in what you do, a content-hungry press can be your best friend. A word of caution: Be prepared to be very diplomatic and to give up control. What people write and say about you is their decision, not yours. You must do your best to be nice and then accept the results, good or bad.

All of these are considered traditional marketing and for each of these there are digital or online counterparts that we will discuss in Chapter 15 on working the Web.

Each of these medium choices has value and you may choose to do only one or two or you may choose to do them all. Be careful here because trying a little of this and a little of that can be expensive. A good policy is to test first. You don't have to mail thousands of pieces. You can test a few hundred at a time. You don't have to buy big ads. You can try small ones first to test the readership. The only exception here is yard signs. You want all the signs you can get.

There is a legend that one of the major national brokerage brands started out in the 1950s as a group of commercial agents. The story goes that they went around their city looking for vacant lots and every time they found one they planted a for-sale sign with their name and number on it. They waited for the owner to call; when they did, they would apologize and ask if the owner wanted to sell. Apparently this got them a lot of listings and launched their business. The funny thing, though, is that some of these owners never called and those signs were up for years making the brokerage name and brand a household word. Of course, you cannot do something like this today without risking arrest but the point is still valid. Signage is powerful.

The Message and the Rules

Now let's look at your other decision—your message. This is where so many agents go wrong. This is where fortunes are squandered. Trying to drive a business with the wrong message or a weak one can empty your pockets long before the results come in. Do not confuse branding, which we discuss in Chapter 16, with message. How you distinguish yourself from all the others is a separate discussion. What we will discuss here applies to all agents and all markets. Here are the six most important rules.

1. It is not about you. It is all about them. Wow, this rule is broken so often it should be a stick-on tattoo you can buy and apply to your chest each morning so you can see it when you brush your teeth. We have a poster in our office that says it another way: "People don't care what you know until they know you care about them." We feel like we should be putting this in all caps like a text message that shouts. Whatever your message is, you need to take out the *I* and put in the *you*. Think about the benefits to your future clients. If you are the number three agent in your office it has no value until you relate it to your potential seller or buyer. Tell them how they are better served by using you. JoAnn has told more clients than I can count that it doesn't matter how many homes we've sold. All that matters is that we sell yours.

2. Start with the relationship and ask for business later. If you only advertise for the transaction, the transaction is all you get. This is why so much effort is wasted running sale ads that bring in enough money to cover the ad and little else. If you have two stores and one is always advertising discounts while the other is advertising service, quality, or a better experience, the first will close in a year and the other will have just begun.

   Let's look at one of the top brands and sellers of merchandisers in the world, Apple. Do they put their computers and digital devices on sale? No. They open stores where you go in and wait for a personal advisor who takes the time to know all about you while building a relationship with you. Always start with the relationship and the business can come later.

3. Spare us another marketing report. Agents do this to death. Marketing reports are everywhere. You slip them off your doorknob when you come home. They are in your mailbox. They pop up on your screen relentlessly and the truth is only a small portion of the public is moved by stats and numbers. The only numbers most people care about are the ones that apply directly to them. How much can I get for my house? How much will this repair cost me? These are the numbers with appeal. Agents spend too much of their budget on marketing information that clients can get anytime, plus the vast majority of clients are not numbers types and could care less. I can say this because I am a numbers person and it is a very lonely thing to be.

JoAnn, on the other hand, falls asleep at the first mention of averages and medians and she has lots of company.

4. Get people to like you by being likable. Speaking of statistics, it is well accepted that people spend their money with people they like. Be personable. Be courteous. Avoid humor because it can just as easily offend as make people laugh.

5. Sell benefits not features. Be the client and ask what's in it for me? The *it* is the feature and the answer is the benefit. When you say the home features five bedrooms to a family of four you may as well be selling ice to Eskimos. Then you point out that the fifth bedroom can be a media room or a home office or a sewing room, you've entered the world of benefits.

6. Finally, don't try to sell more than one thing at once. Just because you are spending the money, don't cram your ads so full in order to average down the cost of each home or message. You see this all the time with multiple-property pages in newspapers and magazines. Unless you only seek to assuage the concerns of sellers who want their home advertised, these are a waste of money. If you must have more than one home on a page, put a border around it to set it apart. Back when we did classifieds, we put our seller's home ad in a box and made the copy longer in order to stand out among the sea of small ads.

If you are marketing a home don't try to make the piece do double duty by saying something about how you would love to market the reader's home as well. Sell the house or sell yourself but don't think you can do both at the same time.

And finally, don't think that just because you've been doing this a long time that you can break the rules. We recently ran a $5,000 ad in a gorgeous magazine and we tried to get readers to ask us home-improvement questions as well as call in for an assessment of their home's value. It was a beautiful ad and we got nothing, nada, zip. Write these six rules down and revisit them often because marketing your message is a slippery slope.

Are these the only rules? Of course not, but they are the ones we see broken all the time. Millions of advertising dollars are wasted each year by agents who have no idea what to do or what their efforts bring them.

Measure Results

As a super agent you must find ways to measure results. Create a coupon or have a contest so you can measure results. Use a dedicated number for responses. Find a way to measure. This brings us to a call to action. You must ask your audience to act. A marketing piece without a call to action is pure immeasurable fluff, the likes of which perfume companies run on television. You want your prospects to act in a way that you can measure. Only by measuring can you know effectiveness. Remember our ill-fated magazine advertisement for two different things: we know it stank because we know we got no action—twice.

Years ago I read about an ad writer who was asked to write a direct-mail piece for a watch seller. The writer wrote an ad for one watch with a choice of three bands. The client called up and said, "I have 20 different watches to sell." After some discussion the ad writer suggested testing two ads to two lists to see which did better. They did and the results were more than surprising. The 20-watch ad received only two inquiries and the single-watch ad received dozens of orders. There are several lessons here. One is that if you want to write your own ads, read books on the subject. The second is that a good test can be invaluable, and the third is that the more choices you give people the less likely they are to be able to make a decision.

Just think about the clients who you've shown a hundred homes to versus the ones you've only shown one or two houses, too. Too many choices lead to indecision.

Speaking of choices, try to limit your marketing to one or two mediums and your message to one or two themes. An agent who only mails postcards and only talks about their ability to stage homes before going on the market is likely to build a sustainable book of business before adding another medium or another message. Test, measure, and get good at a few things before going wild for every new scheme to come down the pike.

Then, when the phone rings, be ready. Have your super powers polished. Put the client first, communicate, motivate, be a professional, and run your practice as an accountable business. You can do this.

Chapter 13 Summary

Only Two Things to Decide

- What is your medium?
- What is your message?
- You cannot delegate these decisions.

(continued)

(continued)

Stay Connected

- Only you know what you want your business to be.
- Stay with what brings you success.
- Think like a superstar.

The Media

- Direct mail.
- Print advertising.
- Signage and outdoor advertising.
- Broadcast, radio, television, and cable.
- Events.
- Publicity.
- Each media choice has a digital counterpart.
- Of all these, signs have the most power.

The Message and the Rules

- It is not about you, it is all about them.
- Start with the relationship and ask for business later.
- Spare us another marketing report.
- Get people to like you by being likeable.
- Sell benefits not features.
- Don't try to sell more than one thing at once.

Measure Results

- You must have a call to action.
- Too many choices cause indecision.
- Limit your focus and get good before you add on.
- Be ready when the phone rings.
- Polish your super powers.

14 Farming

The ultimate form of marketing in real estate is farming. No, we're not talking acreage and a plow. Farming is choosing a fertile area and cultivating its potential clients. Your farm can be based on geography by selecting a particular neighborhood, or demography, by selecting a group of people with a common interest.

We began geographic farming almost from the beginning of our careers. When we signed up with our broker they gave us a hundred business cards. We didn't know a hundred people so I took about half and walked out our front door. I didn't want to talk to anyone because I didn't know what to say so I stuck cards in the closest 50 doorjambs to our house. I actually snuck up and stuck them in the crack and ran like a kid on Halloween. The only enhancement I made was to stamp the backside of the card using the rubber stamp we had for stamping our return address on our bill payments. That small, almost silly, effort led to our first listing when a neighbor walked from two blocks away to knock on our door because she wanted a neighborhood expert. We knew nothing, but her perception was that we did.

The Legend of the Cranberry

Our next effort at farming was at Thanksgiving. We were on a severely limited budget. We bought a case of cranberry sauce on sale with the idea of making a gift for our neighbors. I researched cranberries in a couple of encyclopedias (this was pre-Google times) and wrote a little poem called the *Legend of the Cranberry*. We then took the paper and had a dozen copies made because they were two up on the page. We cut them in half and had a $5^1/_2 \times 8^1/_2$ inch *Legend*. I believe it was on a brownish paper, in keeping with the season. We rolled each of these like little scrolls and tied them with $^1/_8$-inch ribbon and a bow. Then we took business cards, stamped them on the back, and punched a small hole in a corner. Finally we took some more ribbon, threaded it through the hole in the card and between the first ribbon and the scroll, and tied the whole thing around a can of cranberry sauce. I still didn't want to talk to anyone, so once again I snuck the cans onto the closest 24 front porches to our house. How dumb was that? Looking back I can remember how hokey the whole thing looked but not a year goes by that someone doesn't mention those cans of cranberry sauce.

Without knowing what we were doing we accidentally did several things right. As pitiful as the whole thing was, it said we cared to give these neighbors something we made ourselves. It must have been like when your child brings home something from school and you hang it on your fridge. Except that we weren't their child. We were grown people living in the neighborhood. Still, the connection was made on a deeply personal level. Also, we didn't lead with real estate. Yes, our card was a real estate card but the stamped address on the back said we were neighbors. It's like in music, sometimes the pauses between the notes are more important than the notes themselves; the success of our cranberry sauce lay more in what we didn't say than what we did say.

From those early efforts, you might say we were accidental farmers. We had done no research. We didn't know anything about the real estate in our neighborhood. These were just our neighbors and we made an effort to connect.

Our First Farm

Our first purposeful efforts at farming came shortly after Thanksgiving when we decided to send Christmas cards to the almost 1,000 homes in our square mile. We actually live in the southeast corner of that original farm area but it is bordered on four sides by busy boulevards and we called it ours. There are 15 subdivisions in our original farm, with homes ranging from 1,200 square feet to 4,000 square feet, on lots from a quarter acre to a full acre. It is an eclectic mix and about half seem to never move and the other half has about two new listings a week.

We might have been better off just mailing the half who moved often but then we would have missed a lot of business from the other half who, although they seldom moved, had deeper roots in the community and brought us a lot of business in the form of family members and friends. We live in the never-move part of our farm and in 16 years we have probably sold half of the cranberry-sauce houses. That's less than one a year but we can track well over 100 sales from these neighbors who would never even think of using anybody else to serve their real estate needs or the needs of the people they know.

That Christmas we bought boxes of cards from Costco (it was Price Club back then) and while there we found gift tags. There were 48 tags arrayed in 16 groups of three; each group of three was blister packaged (wrapped in shrunken clear plastic) and stuck to large pieces of cardboard. We bought one and took it home and using scissors cut them into 16 little packages of three gift tags each. We went back and bought all they had. Then we went to a couple more stores until we had enough for all the cards.

This time we wrote an even sillier note about how one of the holiday's aggravations was running out of gift tags at the most inconvenient time. We put them all together—card, gift tags, and business cards—and hand-delivered them all because we wanted to save postage. By then we had a small team of six and we each took a section of the farm and stuck them on doors just like I had done before. Our business grew and we've never missed a month sending something to our original farm since.

Market Share

In those early years we expanded from 1,000 to 3,000 and finally to our whole zip code, which includes 15,000 homes. Our zip code regularly produces about 20 real estate closings each week which comes to 1,000 sales a year. This equates to 2,000 transaction sides, because every sale has a buyer and a seller. We have gotten as much as 20 percent of those and never less than 10 percent. When we were concentrating on the smaller groups our market share was higher but never 100 percent. That's why they call it a share, because no one ever gets all the business. So much of the real estate business is fraternal. A member of the family has a license and it would be hurtful not to use them. You are not the only agent working hard.

One of the first things a super agent realizes is that there is plenty of business to go around. An attitude of scarcity, that every client another agent gets is a client taken from you, is a road to paranoia and ruin. Super agents think in terms of abundance. In fact, since so little business is done by average, five-deals-a-year agents, you, as a super agent, couldn't possibly handle all of the business that exists. Plus, you get all those other agents bringing you offers on your listing. Celebrate our industry's bounty and get your share, but don't ever expect to get it all.

One of the advantages you have over us starting out is that you can approach geographic farming more intelligently than we did. You can sit at the computer and research any area. You can determine the velocity of business, how many sales there are annually relative to the number of households, and you can look and see if another agent is dominating the area. We did neither and it worked out pretty well for us, so it should be even better for you.

Geographic Advantages and Economies of Scale

We did have the foresight as we expanded to think about all the advantages geographic farming brought us. First and foremost is signage. If you list 30 homes in the next year over a 20-square-mile area you may get noticed. If you list those same 30 homes in one-square mile everybody notices. People, who have no intention of selling, notice. Buyers, who aren't even looking for an agent, notice. The impact of concentrated efforts is huge.

The next benefit of geographic farming is simple logistics. When the bulk of your business is confined to one area, you drive less and visit more. There are economies everywhere. By concentrating your efforts, you become known quicker and you can focus your advertising dollars on a smaller area and get a larger-than-normal result. Super agents who farm become very well known in their area.

Your connections with other agents who work your area become stronger. You have fewer agents to deal with and build a repeat business with other super agents. Having worked on a previous transaction can do wonders for your clients. Mutual respect and understanding can bring benefits to both sides.

It is amazing the difference market knowledge makes in this business. Now we know that between the Internet, Google, and MLS you can be an expert on any area in less than an hour, but deeply internalized knowledge only comes with repetition and experience. When you spend most of your time in one geographic area you gain knowledge that can't be replicated otherwise. When a house comes on the market and you can say I remember when they sold it two years ago before they put in a pool, that's when your clients are impressed and feel reassured.

Your cost per piece, per postcard, per gift item drops dramatically as your numbers grow. The thing is that the first few copies of any item must also pay for the development and set-up costs. Even though a postcard may cost only three cents to print, the first hundred might have $95 in costs for clip art, copy, and layout. This brings those initial postcards to a dollar apiece, while 5,000 may only cost five cents each.

Expanding

We grew our farm in bits and pieces and we had to make painful decisions along the way. We had growing demand and opportunities to widen our area but with each addition to the numbers we had to make economic decisions. When our farm was 1,000 homes we might spend one or two dollars on each home each month. This ability to go deep with our potential clients brought us a very high return. Ultimately this high return was not enough to feed our growth, so we expanded to 3,000 homes and we turned to bulk mailing to save money.

As we grew more we recognized the potential to expand to almost 15,000 homes but we had to find less expensive giveaways. Today we cover three zip codes and over 30,000 households. Because the increase in business has justified our expansion we have found ever more economical ways to touch the entire area on a monthly basis.

We print our own postcards and greeting cards in-house. We leased a printer the size of a Volkswagon and it seems to stay busy all the time. Because our farm is so large, we now segment our efforts and do different things for different parts of the farm on different timetables. This is also because parts of our farm are modest homes and parts are luxury. As we go forth, we continuously look for opportunities to expand and offer great service to more clients. This consistency of service now takes on a higher role. Also, as we expand and have expanded, there is an additional cost of breaking new ground. This upfront expenditure is like the example given before of McDonald's opening a new restaurant. You have to be ready to launch your expansion as well as continue it after the initial blitz.

Frequency

We have tried more often than once a month and cannot find a justifiable increase in results. We even tried twice a month for a whole year on half our farm and saw no difference in the two halves. Less often is worrisome. So much so that we don't even want to test it. Every year for November and December we don't mail in hopes of covering our large effort to past clients at Christmas. We experience a slowdown but so does our whole market every year around the holidays. All I know is that I feel a big relief when that first Friday in January arrives.

We mail on Fridays because at some point in time we rationalized that Friday was best because with bulk, most people would receive their item on Monday or Tuesday when they are more starved for something to read. There is absolutely no scientific basis for this and we encourage you to establish a schedule that best suits you. Our only admonition would be that whatever you do outside of testing should be consistent. We break our monthly effort into four or five parts and mail every Friday to spread the response evenly over the month.

We would caution you to not move too fast or without some research to base your spending on. A few years ago we added a zip code thinking it would be easy. We had done our examination of the sales activity and it was a winner. What we didn't do was look at who dominated the market. Because this was such an attractive zip code based on volume there were more than a dozen super agents already duking it out with each other. The best any of them had achieved was a $1\frac{1}{2}$ percent market share, which is why we thought it a prime target for expansion. But as our efforts came up short, way short, we got inside the numbers and looked at who else was doing the same thing. They were all top agents. In fact, 10 of the top 25 agents in Arizona were mailing to every person in the zip code. We stopped and spent our money elsewhere.

Geographic farming has been very good for us. Our return on investment is consistently better than $10 for every dollar spent. This return has not come easily or without hiccups along the way but it is lucrative by any standard and this opportunity is just waiting for you. You can be a super agent if you do nothing else but pick 500 to 1,000 homes and become their friend.

Demographic Farming

The realization only came recently to us that we also farmed groups of people. We thought of the mailings and gifts to our past clients as a somehow different thing from our geographic farming. Today we realize that you can farm in many ways other than a plot of ground on a map.

A little over a year ago as our market recovered from the foreclosure fiasco, we knew there would be a shortage of listings until prices recovered enough that people had equity again. One day I asked what was in these two, four-drawer file cabinets in our archive room. I was told they were all the people who didn't list with us over the last 10 years. Now people who call you out to list do not always list. Not with you and not with anybody. But they had it in their mind once so we took the files in those cabinets and made a list. Our criteria were that they were still in the home and not currently listed with another agent. The list had 1,100 names and we started writing a monthly letter to them talking about now being the time to sell. This small farm has produced more than 100 listings in a year.

What kind of list can you put together? If we can find new ways of looking at this business after 15 years of searching, you can people farm overnight. You know your market. You know your trends and statistics. The opportunities in your market are boundless. This is what makes real estate so exciting. You may invent something tomorrow that nobody is doing.

Innovation

If you've been practicing real estate so long that you think it is impossible to innovate, let me give you an example that will blow your mind.

McDonald's became the dominant fast-food burger maker in the 1950s and people at that time thought it was impossible for McDonald's to do more. Their secret was a limited menu, consistently delivered quickly. In the 1960s they invented the Big Mac and increased their business. Over the years, they added more and more stores and increased their business. Then they introduced breakfast and almost doubled their business. Every year they innovate and add to their no-longer limited menu and every year they increase their business. The one that blew me away, however, was the year they started accepting credit cards instead of cash only. That simple innovation to an already world-dominant food empire added billions, that's billions with a *b*, to their business. Now I just saw a commercial advertising their new after-hours menu because in some markets folks just have to have their chicken fingers at three in the morning.

That is innovation and it is free for the thinking. When you start thinking of everything as either prospecting or marketing the picture begins to clear. When you start thinking of any marketing consistently applied to a single geographic area or demographic group as farming, cultivating, and growing customer relationships your vision begins to expand. What if you combine farming with prospecting and start calling or knocking on doors in your farm area? The ideas and innovative possibilities are endless and they are all forms of lead generation.

All That We Do

We are often asked, what do you give or how do you come up with your ideas? Here is a partial list of things we've given and events we've shared. We could probably just revive any of these and start all over again, like painting the Golden Gate Bridge or cleaning the windows of the Empire State Building. Feel free to use these in any way that makes sense to you. Mix them up, combine them, turn them around, and let them lead you to new ideas.

In the past 16 years we've given, mailed, or otherwise used: cranberries at Thanksgiving, pumpkins at Halloween, ornaments at Christmas, gift tags, hot chocolate, popcorn, candy, flower seeds, vegetable seeds, postcards, greeting cards, letters, newsletters, our own newspapers, magnets, mouse pads, movie tickets, lottery tickets, ice cream scoops, Starbucks' coffee, lanterns, Santa's workshop, Tiffany bowls and stemware. We've created various items of value, knowledge, tips, stats, market conditions, encouragement, our seller's success (SOLDs), thank-you notes, handwritten cards, and much more.

If you find yourself stumped for reasons to connect with people here is a list of occasions we have used; New Year's Day, Martin Luther King Day, Groundhog Day, Chinese New Year, Valentine's Day, President's Day, St. Patrick's Day, Easter Sunday, Spring, Tax Day, Administrative Professional Day, Cinco de Mayo, JoAnn's Birthday, Mother's Day, Memorial Day, Flag Day, Father's Day, Independence Day, Labor Day, Back to School, National Grandparents Day, Joseph's Birthday, Columbus Day, Boss's Day, Halloween, Veterans Day, Thanksgiving Day, Pearl Harbor Remembrance Day, Christmas Day, Home Anniversary, His Birthday, Her Birthday, Hanukkah, and New Year's Eve.

Ideas are everywhere. Lists like the preceding ones are mind openers. Once you begin your mind just wakes up and ideas flow. Start making lists today and you may never stop. One day, just maybe, in your endless scribbling and doodling you may come up with a business doubler.

Planning

Just be sure to work ahead. A great idea at the last minute is no idea at all. Marketing takes planning and farming takes scheduling. Calendars follow lists. Lay everything out in a time line. Our favorite is to list the days down the left side of a page or the first column of an Excel spreadsheet. Then you create a column for each thing you plan to do and you fill in start and end dates in the intersecting boxes. If you like, you can really go to town by color-coding, but that's probably only for the obsessive compulsives like me.

About my disorder, just because I overanalyze doesn't mean there's no help. JoAnn has absolutely no interest in creating Excel spreadsheets and she does just fine with planning ahead. We have just learned the hard way and we think, each in our own way, about the future. Planning is essential. If you don't decide where you want to go, you will surely get lost or at the very least go down a lot of dead-end streets. Of all the things you do, marketing and farming, in particular, take planning. You can do this.

Chapter 14 Summary

The Legend of the Cranberry

- Something we made ourselves.
- Did not lead with real estate.
- Made a personal connection.

Our First Farm

- A thousand homes.
- We analyzed volume but it can be misleading.
- Hand-delivered to save postage.

(continued)

(*continued*)

Market Share

- As high as 20 percent and never less than 10 percent.
- Never think scarcity.
- Think abundance.
- You need other agents.
- Don't expect to get it all.

Geographic Advantages and Economies of Scale

- Concentration of signage yields awareness.
- You drive less and talk more.
- Connections become stronger.
- Increased market knowledge.
- Cost per piece goes down.

Expanding

- You have to give up going deep.
- Bulk mail saves big bucks.
- Reduced costs by controlling the process.

Frequency

- We mail monthly but divide it into the four weeks.
- Pick a day and be consistent.
- If an area won't work spend your money elsewhere.

Demographic Farming

- You don't need dirt to farm.
- Think of your past clients as a farm.
- Come up with groups of people to farm.

Innovation

- You don't have to be small to grow big.
- Expand your vision.
- Combine things.

All That We Do

- What we've given.
- When we've given.
- Ideas are everywhere.

Planning

- Work ahead.
- A great last-minute idea is no good.
- Put everything on a calendar.

15 Being Digital

Starting our careers in 1997 gave us front-row seats to the digital transformation of business in general and the real estate profession in particular. As super agents, we experienced the pain and gain firsthand. Over those years the role of the Internet has been tested and retested, defined and redefined, over and over again. Although none of us know with certainty what the future holds, we can offer several conclusions beginning with what the Internet is not.

Promises, Promises

First of all the Internet will not eliminate or do away with the real estate agent. Yes, film, audiotape, and pay phones may be gone. Travel agencies have had a tough existential challenge, but nobody is ready to compare the complexities and the consequences of a real estate transaction to booking a trip to the Bahamas. There are over 2 million agents in this country. Technology is not going to create another 300 million agents so that everybody can do their own transactions. People need representation if only to protect them from themselves.

We have a client who is an attorney who, along with three other attorneys, got together and bought the office building that housed their respective practices. It was a beautiful building and all the tenants were law firms, about 20 in all. Our fearless foursome planned to manage the building. They were, after all, lawyers and on the premises every day.

It would be a piece of cake. For the first five years that our client and his fellow-investor lawyers owned the building, they operated without a single signed lease. Everyone was month to month until they engaged a property management firm to save themselves from each other. Within months all the tenants were on long-term leases save one, and they planned to relocate with the help of a commercial agent.

Our second conclusion is that the Internet and technology in general are not labor- or money-saving devices. The promise was made that these advances would allow us to run our businesses in our pajamas, eating cereal at our breakfast table, while watching our expenses drop to nothing. No way. All we have experienced is faster and easier ways to do ever more work. Simply by virtue of having paperless options we have had to learn them, use them, and keep them updated until a new technology or software comes along that we must learn. If you wish to remain a super agent, which is our preference and where the real money is, then you must hire technological talent. The alternative is for you to become the tech talent and forget about being a good agent first. In addition to the added cost of hardware, software, and talent, the time saved evaporates in a wormhole of infinite options, leaving you to spend every waking hour at your keyboard communing with the world.

Finally, it is not impossible to succeed as a super agent today without any of the modern miracles bestowed upon us daily. An agent needs a smartphone to communicate via voice, text, and e-mail. As recently as 2013 we had breakfast with an agent who was unkind about her peers in a neighboring city. She put the agents in that area down for being behind the times saying they don't want e-mail on their phones because an unhappy client might spoil their day. A super agent needs a branded website if for no other reason than to not look unprofessional. After these two things, the list of must-haves includes a positive and caring attitude, good communication skills, a plan, and the ability to motivate people. Technology and its tools become only as good as you make them. First be a good agent.

Promises Fulfilled

All that said, JoAnn and I welcome every little advance that comes along. Our office supports a 30-agent team and we have four servers housed in their own air-conditioned room, more than 30 workstations (because the marketing department needs both Apple and Windows environments), two giant printers the size of Mini Coopers, and more than 50 flat-screen monitors. Everyone has a smartphone. JoAnn and I have one each, which means, including call waiting, we can be sitting in the car on four calls at once. We have two laptops, two tablets, a stack of legal pads, and cups full of pens everywhere. I counted up software programs we use or have used and reached more than 100 without so much as asking JoAnn what I was forgetting. We welcome every advance and can tell you much that we have learned.

Websites

A super agent we know has a full-time website developer on staff and has created hundreds of sites over the years. Some of these he has today and many were used to address market conditions and then discarded as conditions changed. For instance, during the foreclosure crises he had sites to attract investors and bargain hunters. When Canadians were drawn to the Arizona market he had sites to attract those. He has stealth sites and branded sites. He has wide-area sites and hyper-local sites. He gets leads by the bucketful and gives them to buyer's agents who he hopes can convert them.

Our original website was launched in 2003 and is a dinosaur by today's standards. It cost way too much to develop and even more to maintain. Over the years we just kept adding on and our approach to the changing market has been to come up with URLs to fit the times, give our visitors a landing page, and link them to the right part of our website. We get buyer leads who want to see our listings and we get sellers who want a comparable sales report on their home and we respond as a team.

Aggregators

We buy leads from aggregators such as realtor.com, trulia.com, and zillow.com. These sites and many others like them garner all the listings they can through every source they can, including all the listings on our MLS service. Because they are so large and their search options are so attractive, aggregator traffic is enormous compared to anything you or we could get from our own sites. Most sources agree that 92 to 96 percent of potential buyers begin their search for a home online and these aggregator sites are where they most often start. These leads can vary from immediate to years away, with the majority being in the long-range category. These giant sites then sell the leads to us in the form of a monthly subscription offering us several levels of service.

Some agents act as their own aggregators by creating websites around their local IDX feed from their local MLS. These sites carry hundreds of other agents' listings marketed with the aggregating agent's branding. They are supposed to ask permission from the listing agent, or at the very least remove listings upon request, but many listing agents don't care, reasoning that it is only added exposure for their sellers.

Leads are everywhere. For a price in time, money, or energy, you can have more leads than you can ever hope to handle. Just remember, these leads are only as good as you make them.

Conversion Ratio

You must convert leads to prospects to create value and that conversion is prospecting plain and simple. Whether you get a lead in the form of a text, a call-capture number, an e-mail inquiry, or better yet an e-mail with a phone number, you must contact them back in an effort to begin a conversation that may lead to a relationship. The primary factor here is speed. Internet leads are Internet browsers and the longer they browse after clicking on something that sent a lead to you, the less likely they are to remember where they were in their search and the closer you are to being back to cold calling on the phone. Your goal is to convert an Internet lead to a client from an ever-smaller number of leads. If you convert one in 500 you may as well find another job. If you get it down to one in 50 you are doing well.

Drip, Drip, Drip

Another approach to Internet lead conversion is to capture these people's e-mails and put them on a list that you can send regular e-mails to. This is sometimes called *dripping* or *incubating* but it is actually another form of farming. The reasoning is that these people may be starting to think about real estate or they may be ready right now. By keeping in constant touch, you may be the agent they call when the moment is nigh. E-farming must be much more frequent than monthly—some agents drip daily—because you are now dealing with subject lines, open rates, bounces, and unsubscribes, but if you create compelling content you may be able to harvest business regularly.

Blogging

A good source of content for e-farming can come from postings on your own blog or others blogs. If you are inclined to write regularly about yourself and your market you can develop a higher quality flow of Internet leads. A caution here, if you are not prepared to post often, you may as well save yourself the time. The odds of a single post being highly commented upon or going viral are very long. The only way for you to beat those odds are with volume. If the odds are 1 in 1,000, 10 posts make it 1 in 100 and 100 posts make it 1 in 10. How do you get the big number down from billions to a thousand? Real estate is local and Internet real estate is hyper-local. Just because the whole world is on the other end of your web feed doesn't mean you can sell a condo in Timbuktu. Keep it local and keep it about you and your clients. Blogging is a form of social media and if you only do one thing it is probably the best place to start.

Social Media

The other starting point is Facebook; many agents forego blogging and only do this one thing. The key with Facebook is photos, quotations, and stories. This is not an advertising medium, it is an engagement medium, and the most successful users use it as a communication tool. This requires a constant investment of time but the results can be a strong following of people who feel they know you. The more you learn about the tools offered by Facebook, the more you can get from the site. Take care that you present yourself in a professional as well as friendly light. Social media is today's equivalent of word of mouth. Reputation is everything and today the news travels faster than heat from the sun.

People seek confirmation and reinforcement. They form ideas about things and then they ask others to confirm that they are right. We are all influenced by other people. When you show a home to a prospective buyer, they often want to bring a family member back to reinforce their decision to write an offer. The Internet and social media can do this in a keystroke. Grandma can view a virtual tour a thousand miles away. Technological advances provide marvelous tools. Embrace them.

If you have beautiful photography or video, share them on YouTube. Pinterest, Twitter, Instagram, and Google Plus are all wonderful ways to get out there and connect in the digital world. Find your niche and invest whatever time you wish but first be a good agent and remember your number one goal is to generate leads.

Digital Equivalents

All of the traditional methods of lead generation have a digital equivalent. An e-mail drip campaign can be likened to farming and a virtual tour can be compared to holding an open house. You can be your own media by blogging or podcasting. But for all that is new in technology and on the Internet, the basics of real estate are people and property. Technology can do many things faster or better and often both but in the end you are the super agent. Your super powers of putting the client first, super communication, super motivating, being professional, and running your practice as a business will not be replaced. There is no digital equivalent for putting the client first. You can ask which form of communication a client prefers and then call, text, or e-mail accordingly. You can probably even put the question into a computer program and have it asked automatically but it is you who will compose that communication. It is you who will use the most powerful computer of all, the one between your ears. You are the super agent.

Chapter 15 Summary

Promises, Promises

- The Internet will not do away with the real estate agent.
- The Internet and technology in general are not labor- or money-saving devices.
- It is not impossible to succeed as a super agent today without any of the modern miracles bestowed upon us daily.

Promises Fulfilled

- We welcome advances.
- We buy hardware.
- We buy software.

Websites

- Some agents have many websites.
- We have one site and many URLs.
- We all get leads.

Aggregators

- 92 to 96 percent of people begin their search on the Internet.
- Big sites attract many leads.
- They sell them to us relatively cheap.

Conversion Ratio

- Lead conversion to a valid prospect is prospecting.
- You must be fast.
- You must have a low ratio to make it worth the time.

Drip, Drip, Drip

- This is e-farming.
- You must be more frequent.
- You must offer content.

Blogging

- Higher-quality leads.
- You must post often.
- Keep it local.

Social Media

- Facebook is photos, quotations, and stories.
- Facebook is an engagement tool.
- Be professional.

(continued)

(*continued*)

- People seek confirmation and reinforcement.
- Find your niche.

Digital Equivalents

- All traditional methods of lead generation have a digital equivalent.
- Your super powers will not be replaced.
- You are the super agent.

16 Branding

I can do that, too. I can give you your own website, too. I can put you on that tour, too. I can cut my commission, too. We can all do this. We can all do that. Why don't we all get together and form a real estate union so people can just call up and order an agent from the union hall? We are, after all, interchangeable robots with the same few hours of education and a license from our state agency. Sound silly? Just look around you.

Listen to what people are saying. "I need an agent for the paperwork," as if any agent will do. "I wasn't sold yet, so I switched agents," as if we were like socks with plenty more in the drawer. "I'm trying to decide who to give the commission to," as if our earnings were an undeserved gift. No wonder new agents get asked to cut commission all the time. If you are not a valued professional, you are a commodity, and the only way to be a valuable professional is to be a brand.

A brand sets you apart, makes you unique, and insures that you get paid what you ask.

Your Name

When JoAnn and I got our first listing, we needed to run an ad. I looked in the newspaper. It still had classifieds back then and I scanned the pages for ideas. There were several agent couples working our area at that time and they all used "The" preceding their last names. There were "The Johnsons" and "The Hamptons" and some others that all looked similar. I bounced around a few possibilities and came up with "Those Callaways." It stuck. In fact, it was sticky. People found it catchy. They remembered it.

This was our first effort at branding. Had I chosen "Them Callaways" we might have been branded as a little backwoodsy or "These Callaways" might have come off a little self-centered. I put "That Callaway" on JoAnn's phone for a while but then she made me take it off. You do need to use some care in choosing your message. Think about how it will be received. If it appeals to your clientele but may offend others, you will have to decide the value of the trade-off. We suggest you remain inclusive to all.

In becoming unique, you can start with your name or you can create a tag line. If your name is John Blake or Beth Thompson, you can make it more memorable with the casual Johnny or Betty. You can go more formal with Jonathan or Elizabeth. If your family called you Jack or Lizzy, you might want to consider these. If your friends in college tagged you with Jon Jon or Puffy, one of these may set you apart. Another approach is the inserted nickname, as in John "Johnny" Blake or Beth "Lizzy" Thompson. All of these serve as a first consideration when branding.

You want to give this careful consideration because your name stays with you and is not easy to change. In fact, your name can change you. All my life I was Joe until I met JoAnn. She said she preferred Joseph and my life was forever changed.

Another twist on naming is where people change letters to make the spelling more unique. They change Mary to Mari or Tim to Tym. These conventions can be tricky and lead more to misspelling than memorability but if your mother named you Debee, so be it.

Alliteration is very memorable. The master of this was Richard Nixon's vice president before Gerald Ford, Spiro Agnew. He would often coin complete alliterative sentences of 5 to 10 words all starting with the same letter. Peter Piper picked a peck of pickled peppers may be a tongue twister but it is also something you can never forget. Bobbie Baxter is more memorable than Roberta Baxter. William Winters is more memorable than Bill Winters.

Tag Lines

If you already have an alliterative, catchy, or memorable name or if you like your name just fine, you might try a tag line. Sometimes called *catch phrases* because they catch people's attention, tag lines can identify you and quantify you. Also, tag lines are easily changed. You can shed the old and put on the new with a keystroke and a printer.

Some agents reason that branding can narrow their focus and prequalify their clients. Take care not to pigeonhole yourself. Bradford Farms Specialist may get you clients who have their hearts set on Bradford Farms, but these same prospects might question your capabilities elsewhere.

Tag lines can establish your specialty, your geographic area, your personality, anything you like. You can even have different tag lines for different situations. For buyers you might use, "Fulfilling your dreams" and for sellers, "Getting you moving," although I would hope you can do better than these quick examples.

Our first tag line came from narrowing down a much longer paragraph. JoAnn wanted something for a postcard that said we would get our sellers sold. I wrote about 300 words and she said make it shorter. We went back and forth several times and I got it down to "When you want to move, call us and we will get you sold." JoAnn shook her head and said it wasn't catchy, so I thought about it some more. At the time we had sold maybe a dozen homes in our area and the first sale we made I had bought a rider, a smaller sign to hang under the main sign that said "Sold in ___ days." We used a grease marker to put a five in the space. We thought the five days was impressive but it wasn't nearly as strong as the second sale we made. For this one we had a 6 × 18 inch rider made with just the word SOLD in five-inch, bold letters. This rider made the phone ring. I thought about this and realized the phone rang because the callers wanted to be sold too. That's when we came up with, "When you want a SOLD sign . . ." The three dots implied more and, of course, most people add in their heads "call Those Callaways" to finish the phrase. At least we hope they do. Anyway, we trademarked it and copy protected it and we've used it for 15 years and it seems to work. Is it the only tag line in the world? Of course not. You may come up with something incredible and when you do, protect it and use it because it makes you unique. It brands you.

Your Look

Once you have decided on a unique use of your name or a tag line or both, you need to decide on your look. We're not talking about your haircut or makeup or wardrobe. You need to be you. Trying to be anybody or anything else other than who you are is a road to failure and disappointment. You are already unique. Do not change. How you present yourself to your clients, however, is something over which you have total control and you want to give it careful consideration. Everything you do is part of your look.

Start with your e-mail. What font is you? What font size is you? What does your e-signature look like? Do you have a logo? If you are going to have and be a brand, if you are going to set yourself apart from the crowd, be respected as a professional, and get paid in full for what you offer, you need to think about these details.

Logos are simple things. You might sketch yours on a napkin in five minutes or you might hire an expert, but in the end it is more important what you do with a logo than what it imparts. A logo steps you up and separates you from all those who do not have one.

Many agents use their photo or headshot as their logo. This is very popular and some experts extol the virtue of the power look, where you seem to be staring into the viewer's very soul. You are certainly unique, so your photo fulfills that requirement as a logo, but beware the pitfalls. Everyday, we see high school graduation photos on the business cards of agents with grandchildren. If you want your face to be the logo, make it the one you wear today and update it regularly.

We know an agent who stepped this up to the next level and ran ads with all her headshots from over the years. It worked for her because she projected experience and a comfort with herself that others were attracted to. She was also the exception and you can use your own imagination as to how photos of one's self may be abused.

Massive Action

Whichever route you take, logo or photo, you must put it everywhere. We call this massive action and it serves to identify all you do. Your first considerations in putting yourself everywhere are colors and consistency. Your broker may dictate certain colors or may have color criteria so check first. Whatever you do, you want it to be in compliance with your broker. Even if your broker has a main color combination, you may be allowed to use secondary colors or shades of the main colors.

Our colors are navy blue, yellow, and white. These were the colors of our original broker and while the blue remained constant, our broker's yellow went through a number of mutations while he allowed us to stick with the original. After 12 years, our broker merged with a larger operation and their colors were gold on black. We decided at that time to form our own brokerage and became an independent operation. The public didn't even notice because our colors remained the same.

Colors weren't our only consideration in making such a big change but it was an important part of our decision and you may be faced with the same choices if you change brokers. For us, becoming a brokerage was a huge step. It is not something we would recommend for everyone. Most agents need the guidance of a good broker. Your broker already has branding, although it is not yours, but it is something you can build on. Your broker is your mentor, your protector, and sometimes even your savior. Try to pick your broker well and stay with the same one because even more than colors or name or tagline is consistency.

Consistency

Even bad ideas consistently applied have great power. Communism is a good example. You have to abhor their methods but you must admire their consistency. They never budged an inch on what was known as the party line until Mr. Gorbachev softened and it all came tumbling down. Coca-Cola has used the same font for years. You just know there have been dozens of young guns with new logo ideas for the executives in Atlanta, but they said no to change. Coke has remained consistent, and today they are number one in the world and Diet Coke is number two. This is power.

JoAnn and I debated that consistency should be a super power but in the end decided not to list it as such because we have seen great success reinvent itself over and over again. The five super powers of putting the client first, communication, motivation, professionalism, and accountability are not optional. No true success is achieved without having or hiring all five of these super powers. But consistency is an option you should consider because it can make the mediocre successful and the talented super successful.

We put our name and our tag lines (we have several) everywhere. Here is just a partial list of where we brand ourselves in yellow and blue:

Every newspaper ad, magazine ad, postcard, handout, greeting card, enclosure card, thank-you card, birthday card, business card, flyer, brochure, and our letterhead stationary on paper and in e-mail, has one consistent look. Our yard signs, riders, directional signs, open house signs, posters, placards, and any outdoor advertising is yellow and blue.

Everything we do online, on our websites, our blogs, our Facebook, Twitter, Instagram, Google Plus, and more has a consistency that gives it power.

Be an Expert

For most agents, having a catchy name or tag line, a logo or great headshot, and a consistent look consistently applied is enough to set them apart and give them a brand. How far you take it from here is up to you. The next step up is to position yourself as an expert. If you are an expert, people come to you with a new respect. They respect your time and they respect your money. An expert seldom gets asked about their fee or their commission. There is an old saying that says if you have to ask the price, you cannot afford it. This is the respect an expert receives.

When you are an expert people ask if you have the time. They appreciate your time and it becomes easier for you to protect your time. Being an expert isn't where the money comes from. The money comes from serving your clients at the highest level and applying your super powers. But being an expert can make everything easier and more enjoyable. Just remember that you weren't born an expert. It is something to which you strive and you should appreciate its achievement every day. An arrogant expert is a turnoff and will destroy everything else you've built. Seek humility and your success will be multiplied.

Before you position yourself as an expert, take the time to become one. We have seen many agents proclaim their expertise and skip this step entirely only to be found out and suffer sometimes irreparable damage to their reputations. Whatever you choose as an expertise, choose wisely. Realize that you must pay the price. You must read the materials. You must attend the seminars, conferences, meetings, lunches, and networking events that put you in touch with people who can add to your expertise. Only when you feel you have a contribution to make can you consider yourself to be an expert.

When you are ready to make that contribution to the world, when you are ready to declare yourself an expert, there are many avenues you may take to proliferate yourself and your brand as an expert. Just be sure that whatever road you take, you do it humbly and let your consistent messaging establish your expert status rather than you proclaiming your position and then having to constantly prove your claims. Alternatives to saying you are an expert are many. You can be a source. This is inviting. People need a source. You can be an advisor. People often seek advice. You can be a mentor, an authority, anything but an expert. Let others proclaim you as an expert and you will find acceptance without resistance.

What to Do

The easiest street to expert status is a newsletter. What makes this easy is that you don't even have to write it yourself. It is better if you do—at the very least you should be involved in guiding or approving its content—but a newsletter's power is in its consistency. You can also do a newsletter on anything. You can choose a geographic newsletter to go with your farming efforts or you can make it on home improvements. The possibilities are endless. You can deliver a newsletter electronically, by mail, or even hand them out door to door. The options are limitless and all newsletters succeed in time.

You can start a blog or contribute to other's blogs. Again, this can be hired but your audience will believe it is you and you will have to be accountable to your content. Blogging, tweeting, Instagram—these forms of messaging are personal and require your involvement. Insincerity online stands out like a cruise ship in a small port.

If you enjoy public speaking or think you might be able to learn, you can make yourself available for panel appearances. You can participate in events. You can be an announcer, an instructor, a presenter, or even the keynote speaker. These experiences can greatly enhance your expert status.

You may even write a book or write one with the help of a professional writer. A book today has almost become a business card. A book can gain you audience that is unlike any other.

You can make videos. YouTube has given every individual a channel to express himself or herself. Again, the keys are knowing what you are talking about and consistency.

Be the News

Publicity is a double-edged sword because you never know how the press is going to use your words. If you can articulate your message well in a form that is not easily misinterpreted or misused, a reporter can help you gain expert status. You can court this exposure a number of ways. One is to call up different media and pitch your idea on something newsworthy. The key here is brevity and a good idea. Remember, these are hard-working individuals in need of content, but respect their need for good content. Don't sell sameness in your stories or ideas. Give them a fresh look or a different way of looking at something. Another approach, if your strength is on paper, is the press release. Here you have an opportunity to more fully develop ideas than the elevator pitch might limit. Your recipient list need not be every media source in a hundred-mile radius, although that approach can work, because your goal is to get one or two people who like your ideas to keep coming back for more. Get interviewed and be newsworthy. Just remember that this is a branding opportunity and you need to get in who you are, what your tagline is, and how you want to be remembered. Much will be filtered out but some will remain and your status as an expert will grow.

Someone said either you are known for something or you will be known for nothing. Branding is your opportunity to decide who you want to be, what you want to be known for, and how you are perceived. It is exciting. You actually get to sit down and think about it and come up with whoever you want to be and then be that person. Go ahead. Invent yourself.

The Cumulative Effect

Then, put yourself everywhere. The incredible thing about branding is the cumulative effect. We were in business maybe two years when JoAnn and I had to go downtown to pick up tickets we had reserved for a concert. I think it was Cher or Tina Turner. The arena has no curbside parking, so I let JoAnn off and went around the block. When I got back, she was waiting and waving both hands. She got in and almost couldn't talk she was so excited. "Guess what happened?" she said and I just looked dumb waiting for more. "I gave the girl our last name and she asked if I was one of Those Callaways!"

I was amazed. Outside our family, it seemed like nobody knew who we were. Yes, we had sold a lot of homes in northeast Phoenix but this was downtown. I asked if the girl lived in our zip code and JoAnn shook her head explaining that she had asked and the girl said no, she just liked our ads in the *Arizona Republic*.

At that time we had run ads in the Sunday real estate section maybe 100 times. Today that number is over 1,000 and we get asked, "Are you Those Callaways?" all the time and I have to admit, it is just as thrilling today as it was that first time. We so appreciate the recognition and the opportunities our branding brings us.

You can do this. You can invent yourself and put yourself out there and be consistent. You can differentiate yourself from the crowd. Don't just be another real estate agent.

Be the agent who is known for something or somewhere. Be your brand and see the fruits of your super labors multiplied again and again. You can do this.

Chapter 16 Summary

Your Name

- Stand out by differentiating yourself.
- Make your name unique.
- Spelling, nicknames, and alliteration.

Tag Lines

- Easily changed.
- Narrows your focus.
- Establishes specialty.

Your Look

- Your e-mail font.
- Your e-mail signature.
- Your logo or photo.

Massive Action

- Importance of color.
- Be broker compliant.
- Think twice before changing.

Consistency

- Even bad ideas consistently applied have great power.
- Not a super power because it is optional.
- Everything we do is more powerful because of consistency.

(*continued*)

(continued)

Be an Expert

- Experts get more respect.
- They get paid.
- Do the work.
- Stay humble.
- Let others proclaim your expertise.

What to Do

- Publish a newsletter.
- Write a blog.
- Public speaking.
- Have a book.
- Make videos.

Be the News

- Publicity is a double-edged sword.
- Brevity—have an elevator pitch.
- Press release allows fuller explanation.
- Get one or two media contacts.
- Invent yourself.

The Cumulative Effect

- It all adds up.
- It is a thrill.
- Be your brand.

Super Time Management

"Don't wait. The time will never be just right."
> —Napoleon Hill, author of *Think and Grow Rich*

"This time, like all times, is a very good one, if we but know what to do with it."
> —Ralph Waldo Emerson

"That's right—time is for sale."
> —Chapter 17, page 165, *Super Agent*

17 Time Is More Than Money

It has been said that time is money. More accurately, time is like money. Time, like money, is an intangible. You can't see it, feel it, or touch it. Oh, you can hold a watch or set a clock but these are only tangible representations of time, just as you can count your tens and twenties, but those pieces of paper really have no value until the government says they do.

Just look at all the ways we describe time in which we can just as easily replace the word time with the word money. We can spend time, save time, lose time, keep time, waste time, make time, take time, find time, buy time, sell time, budget our time, ask for more time, have limited time, have time on our hands, or be out of time. But blood money doesn't work and it would be a leap to describe inherited time. Time and money diverge in a number of ways.

You cannot switch out time for money when you set a time or pass time or it's high time, party time, the first time, the last time, the right time, the wrong time, a good time, a bad time, an easy time, a hard time, crunch time or one more time. Soldiers serve their time. Prisoners do time. Real estate agents are told to block their time and for most of us we have no idea what that means.

Money Is a Problem

Money is like time but no one is suggesting that money is time. Time is unique. But here is an interesting similarity between time and money that you may not have thought of.

161

A wise investor we respect once said, "Money is a problem." You have no money, it's a problem. You have too little money, that's a problem. You have just enough money so you wish you had more. You have more money and you save or spend it and wish you had even more. Ultimately, you have more money than you can spend and you have a whole new set of problems. What do you do with all this money? Do you help anyone who asks? If you give away too much you might not have enough anymore. Money is always a problem.

We watched an interview on the *Oprah* show. She was sitting in Edinburgh, Scotland talking with J. K. Rowling, the author of the Harry Potter books, and the subject of success came up. Oprah asked Ms. Rowling if she worried about money and she said every night she feared it would all disappear the next day, to which Oprah replied, "Me, too." Here we were, watching two of the world's richest, self-made women, both billionaires, and they each admitted to never feeling comfortable with wealth. Money was a problem.

Time Is a Problem

As JoAnn and I talk to agents all around the country we find time is a problem and most folks fall into two groups: agents with too much time, ("What do I do next?") or agents with too little time ("I have no life"). There is a third group, however, and these are the super agents for whom time is not a problem. Let's talk about that.

Years ago Elizabeth Dole ran for president. It was a short-lived campaign. Her husband was Bob Dole, the senator, and she had held a cabinet post, and the Republicans were struggling with too many candidates. Elizabeth was a lovely southern lady and she had an endearing accent. A reporter was interviewing her and asking question after question—How would you solve this and how would you solve that? Finally, Elizabeth in her infinite wisdom said, "Darlin', you have to understand. We don't solve problems in Washington, we manage them."

A lightbulb went on and JoAnn and I have been managing ever since. We stopped trying to solve everything and found that if you manage anything long enough it solves itself.

Around year three in our real estate careers we hit the wall. We were getting up at 6 a.m. and making our list for the day which was always impossible to complete. As if by magic, our cell phone started ringing at eight and if we hadn't yet showered and dressed, calls could delay us by up to an hour. We had a team of 10 and they were already busy when we arrived at the office. Our days were one long listing appointment interrupted by trips back to and from the office, during which we negotiated contracts, created marketing, solved everybody's issues, and made calls. We worked until 9 or 10 p.m., completing 16-hour days, and we did it every day of the week, racking up 112-hour weeks. We took no vacations. We didn't even take a day off. Were it not for our relationship, one or both of us would have burned out and thrown in the towel.

Then I heard Elizabeth Dole on the radio, and it all began to change. When we began to manage problems rather that forcing a solution, we began to look at our time differently. Perhaps we could take control of something that up to now seemed impossible, by simply changing how we looked at it and by looking for ways to manage our time.

Hunger

Early in our marriage—our girls were near nine, eight, and five—we found ourselves without permanent employment and going from odd job to odd job with a little self-employment thrown in. We bought a set of brass stencils, a paint roller, a can of white latex paint, and a can of black spray paint. We went door to door in neighborhoods that had curbing and offered to paint the street number on the curb in black on a white background. As I said, these were odd jobs. Because money was so tight, we committed to writing down every penny in a daily journal in hopes of understanding where the money went. We did this religiously for six months and learned something very surprising. When you are living hand to mouth, every minute of the day is consumed with food. We didn't eat out. We didn't buy groceries once a week. We got up in the morning. We painted some curbs. We went to the store. We came home and ate. We ate a lot of macaroni and cheese at 21 cents a box and navel oranges at 10 cents a pound. Our hunger drove us and consumed our time.

When we started our real estate careers we were hungry to pay our bills. We owed money and that was a powerful motivator. As the bills got paid, we stayed hungry. This kind of financial success was new to us. It was exhilarating and we craved more. When we got near the breaking point from work, work, work, we decided to reevaluate our goals. We needed the success but we needed to have a life as well. We decided to take some evenings off and to go for Sunday drives. We changed our hunger. We modified our appetite and our management of time followed.

When the world failed to explode on Sundays, we set about to carve more time off into our schedules and in the process get more out of the time that remained for work.

This was all a conscious effort. We had made the decision. We had a new goal. We had a new hunger.

Arnold Schwarzenegger's first movie was about bodybuilding and it was titled *Stay Hungry*. In it he tried to explain the sacrifices he made to build his body. He talked about the constant dieting but he also created a metaphor about life and goals. He said that to achieve his dreams of being Mr. Olympia, he had to stay hungry. Today, Arnold has achieved his success, made his movies, governed California, and returned to Hollywood to make more movies. Arnold never stopped being hungry. He is hungry today.

What Are You Hungry For?

Hunger here has been used as a replacement for goals. Setting goals sounds so bland but when you think about hunger, your needs become clear. When you talk about cravings, you feel your goals physically. What are you hungry for?

What does hunger have to do with time management? Everything. A super agent knows that time is not money. Time is the measure of our lives. Time is the great equalizer. Unlike money we all get the same 24 hours in a day, the same 7 days in a week, the same 52 weeks in a year. No one gets more. No one gets less, provided they live out the year, which is never a certainty. Time is a unique concept. Time is intangible but very real, and how we treat it is more important than anything because time is much more than money, and for a super agent time becomes a craving.

There is a big difference between having eaten an hour ago and not eating for three days. Hunger and satisfaction are a function of food and time. You wouldn't think of going through life not knowing where your next meal is coming from, yet many of us have no idea what we want to accomplish. We just go along reacting to demands on our time. What if you treated food that way? I'll just go along and eat whatever I'm given. Sounds ridiculous doesn't it? You need to decide what you want and go after it. Hunger for your goals and time will manage itself.

Buy Time

Back in Chapter 1, we told you that super agents make more and work less. We also told you that super agents were super accountable. Part of that accountability, managing your practice like a business, is to manage your time. You must know your numbers and you must know your schedule. You must also know your capacities and not overextend yourself financially or physically. A super agent knows this and looks for ways to buy time. That's right—time is for sale.

When you got your first job, you probably sold your time for wages. This means someone was buying your time for those wages. Time is bought and sold every day. Do you think the president of the United States is doing it all by himself or herself? No. The entire executive branch of our government is serving at his or her pleasure and he or she gets it all done and still finds time to go to Camp David. A super agent realizes that one of the things their extra money makes possible is the purchase of time to make things easier. How much time you buy and how much easier you want things to be is up to you. You must make the budget decisions based on what you want.

Once we changed our goals from just the money to the time to enjoy it, JoAnn and I went from overload to almost no load. Our business funds our life and we gladly pay for the freedom it brings. How did we get there? That is what the rest of this book is about. We decided on what we wanted and then we hungered and craved it until we had it. Along the way were a thousand small decisions—who to hire, what to advertise, where to take our business—but our hunger never waned and we were never sated. We hunger today.

Manage Your Energy

A super agent understands energy and understands how to manage it. Human energy can be likened to the electricity in a battery. Each morning we get up with a full charge and proceed to deplete ourselves throughout the day. If we are in stressful situations, we use up our charge at a faster rate. If we idle away an hour, we may use no energy or we may even charge ourselves up a little because sleep is not the only way we gain energy. Rest, relaxation, time off, vacation, all these charge us up. Work, talking to clients, negotiating, getting a deal closed, solving situations use up energy. You must manage your energy.

Agents who fail to manage their energy are like road warriors we see at the airport with their laptops and smartphones plugged in between planes. Have you ever tried to have a conversation with someone whose phone is on its last 10 percent of charge? That's what trying to do business is like when you fail to manage your energy. You get down to the end of your battery life and you find yourself constantly trying to get a quick charge until your next bad connection when you try to find a little more energy to get you through the day. Take a day off. Make managing your energy a part of your hunger. Write it down. Plan for it. Your business should serve you, not the other way around.

Get Off the Treadmill

What about all those distractions and commitments? What about all the things that eat up your day, the other agents who want to tell you about their deal that fell through, the family members who need you to fulfill their needs? What about all the unimportant urgencies that get in the way of you addressing the important issues that are not pressing matters? How do you get off the treadmill where everything is important and due right now? How do you protect your time and make yourself effective?

Can you simply hunger for all these to go away? Do you just throw money at these obstacles to your success? Do you ultimately pace yourself and hope to have enough energy to do it all? Perhaps, but the answer to distractions or over commitment lies in prevention rather that treatment. The answer lies in the power of no.

When you hunger for time to have a life, you must say no to the people and things that would suck you dry and rob you of life's most precious gift. Make time your first priority and when you have it as truly yours to spend, then you can decide if that agent's tale of woe is important to you or if that family member is who you want to spend your time on.

When you buy time, you must say no to the projects that are simply not worth the money. You must do away with all that is not urgent or important and then you must spend your money on reducing urgency because money spent rashly is money often misspent.

When you manage your energy you must say no to commitments that will drain your reserves. Take care not to serve two masters. Gain that level of energy that comes from under commitment and then enjoy doing what you choose.

What to Do Next

What about the other side of the problem? What about agents who have nothing but time? What about those who don't know what to do next? Some might say that people who don't know what to do with their time are lazy or simply not bright enough to schedule themselves. Nothing could be further from the truth. For these agents, the answer to what to do next, lies in the question: What are you hungry for?

If you are not hungry, you are sated. You may as well take a nap. That's what lions do. For all their ferocity, lions hunt, lions eat, and lions lay in the grass, satisfied. People are seldom lazy. They are more often satisfied or resigned to their current state. If this is you, then ask yourself what you are hungry for.

If you are still wondering what to do first, go back to Chapter 3 and work on making your next deal. Go back to Part II and work on lead generation. Any time you are not talking to a client and working on a deal, you should be lead generating.

If you want to be a super agent, get hungry and stay hungry. Use that abundance of time to learn the fundamentals and to become a lead-generating client magnet, and when you run out of that abundance, change your hunger from money to time and you will have become a super agent.

You can do this.

Chapter 17 Summary

Money Is a Problem

- Not enough.
- Want more.
- Too much.

Time Is a Problem

- Don't solve problems, manage them.
- Manage a problem long enough and it goes away.
- Our problem was not enough time.

Hunger

- Hunger consumes time.
- Manage your hunger.
- Stay hungry.

(continued)

(*continued*)

What Are You Hungry For?

- Your needs become clear.
- Time is much more than money.
- Where is your next meal coming from?

Buy Time

- Time is for sale.
- The president buys time.
- Pay for freedom.

Manage Your Energy

- Like electricity in a battery.
- Don't get down to your last 10 percent charge.
- Take a day off.

Get Off the Treadmill

- The power of no.
- Say no to distractions.
- Say no to commitments.

What to Do Next

- Too much time.
- Hungry or sated?
- Change your hunger from money to time.

18

Allies, Affiliates, and Vendors

"**N**o one succeeds alone."

JoAnn wants to kill the guy. We are at an annual conference held by one of the largest real estate franchises in the country and our host has about 80 nonfranchisee agents in a breakout session obviously designed to recruit us to their brand. This is fine with us because the conference offers so much to learn and because of the respect we have for our host who is one of the brightest minds in our industry.

Now this guy disagrees with our host. He says he is number one in his market, which is a major Pacific Coast city, and he says, "I do. I do it all by myself."

I restrain JoAnn by gently squeezing her hand for fear she may pounce on the guy from across the room or at the very least, jump up and give him what only JoAnn is capable of. I mumble something about leaving it to our speaker and what follows is an excruciating display of denial and irrationality that goes on for almost the entire allotted hour. At the end, JoAnn is squeezing my hand in restraint.

This idiot carries on a debate with this genius who is a model of outward calm and who I'm sure inwardly holds the same homicidal urges as the rest of us and in the end this agent is still convinced that he does it all alone and that his success is his alone. Much of the discussion revolves around Michael Jordan and how in this man's opinion, Michael succeeded alone. It is as if Michael had no coaches, no teammates, no fans. For that matter, in this guy's opinion, Michael didn't even need an opponent to score against. Michael Jordan became the greatest basketball player of his time all alone.

Finally, after ruining the session for everybody the bozo shuts up, a couple of agents stand up and say how they are going to sign up for a franchise and we go back to our hotel.

What is so striking about this memory, what makes it vivid, is the absurdity of that agent's denial and belief in his own independence. Yes, ours is an industry of independent contractors but we depend on each other every minute of every day. Yet here he was, saying how he was number one, and that he did it all on his own. Let's only hope that our industry will be purged of this arrogance to be replaced with an appreciation for all who support our efforts and who we support in return.

Other Agents

Just as Michael Jordan could not rise to the top without other players, we cannot succeed without other agents. Sure, we compete for listings and we each represent our respective clients in a transaction, but we need each other to expand our inventory available to our buyers and to expand our buyer pool for our sellers. We need each other to support our associations and protect our code of ethics. We need each other to preserve our profession from pressures to dismantle our industry into the hands of attorneys, banks, or the government. As real estate agents we provide a deeply personal service that protects our clients through the legal minefield and we do it more than 10 million times a year with an unbelievably high degree of success. Without us our courts would be jammed, the cost of home ownership would rise, and the American Dream would more often than not turn into a nightmare. Think about this. Look in the mirror, give yourself a pat on the back, and when you talk to the next agent you encounter, treat them with the respect they deserve. No one succeeds alone.

At Those Callaways, JoAnn says we are a haven to other agents. When we get a call from an agent who is out of town or otherwise cannot show their client our listing, we meet the clients for them and respect their agency. When we get an agent on the other side of a transaction, who is obviously inexperienced or seldom does a deal, we help them along. When we see an agent who is forgetting an important detail, we remind them. We believe that what goes around comes around and our business is local and our community of agents is therefore relatively small and that if we treat other agents well, we will be treated well in return.

Our legal system is described as adversarial and some people mistakenly take that as being somehow like warfare rather than a debate seeking justice. Politicians often have to remind us that they are only running against an opponent, one who holds an opposite view. Politics is no place for hateful rhetoric. Some agents need to understand that representation is not argumentation and that advocacy can be a civil exercise. As a super agent you must commit to courtesy at all times. Say please and thank you. Allow others to express their view. Remove judgment. Don't interrupt. Say "Excuse me" when you must and apologize quickly when you are wrong, for none of us are perfect. You don't get along by going along. You get along by leading with good manners and setting an example for others.

Title and Escrow

An affiliate is someone with whom you share a client, and your number one affiliate relationship is with your title company or escrow provider. An escrow officer is hired by one or both of the parties to act as an independent third party to represent the terms of the contract. In this role they share your buyer and/or seller with you. They also deal with the buyer's lender, sharing the client there as well. Then there are all the other parties hired by either the buyer or seller. In some states lawyers are involved. The government has a stake in seeing that taxes are paid and title is properly recorded. At the center of all this is the escrow officer. They are necessary. Sometimes they are saviors but they are not your client's new agent. Do not abdicate your role and simply say call me when the check is ready. Your clients need you now more than ever and if you do not stay at the center of the transaction someone else will gladly take your place.

Remember that, as the agent, you create the transaction that all these other people serve. You are the source of their business but you must be a good source. You cannot throw together flawed contracts and expect the escrow officer to sort it out.

As an agent you will develop relationships with certain escrow officers and will prefer that your transactions go through them. This is sometimes possible if your client agrees but over time you will deal with many escrow officers because other clients and other agents also have their own preferences. Treat these affiliates well because you need their goodwill for your client.

Your preferred escrow provider, however, can be a wonderful ally in your business. They can offer you assistance in marketing. They can access information unavailable on your MLS system. They can speak well of you to your clients and they can advocate for you and for your client.

Affiliate Power

I'll tell you what one escrow manager did for us. We had a client call on a Tuesday to say she had lost her home the day before. We had sold her the home ten years prior and she didn't know who else to call. She said that she had been trying to get a loan modification and that on Friday she was told her application was denied and the home would be auctioned on Monday. She told the bank she could get the money from her father to pay the loan current and was told it was too late. She also said her mother was in the home in hospice care and again was told it was too late. On Monday her mother passed away and the trustee sold the home to a third party, a gruff remodeler who was now banging on our client's door.

Enter Allison, our escrow manager. When JoAnn told Allison of this travesty, Allison made it her mission to talk to the right person at the bank and e-mailed every executive of the bank above the status of teller. By the end of the week she had the bank president on the line and when she said, "You probably don't know who I am," he said, "Oh, yes I do."

Between Allison and JoAnn the bank made several offers, each one better than the last and in two weeks our client had her home conveyed back to her with a new smaller loan and the gruff contractor had been paid $50,000 for his trouble. That's the power of a strong affiliate relationship.

Your Preferred Lender

Sometimes you will engage with a client after they have already begun a relationship with a lender but more often your buyer will look to you for a recommendation. Treat this responsibility with the utmost of attention and concern. You may have found a lender who is one size fits all or you may have several lenders whom you know and feel confident in recommending. Be sure you give your client the best possible person you know for their needs.

A super agent knows as many lenders as possible. When you represent a seller you are dependent on that buyer's lender being able to perform. Respect their client relationship and do everything possible to maintain a positive communication with the loan officer. Your client is relying on you.

As a super agent you must understand that lenders have a very difficult role to play in a transaction. They are trying to do their very best for their client while dealing with company guidelines, underwriters, appraisers, and any number of other issues relating to the property and the borrower's credit and capacity to get a loan. Lenders are constantly bombarded with requests to stretch here and push there. On top of all that, they have the seller and seller's agent, who are not their client, asking to be privy to every detail in an effort to be assured of closing. Theirs is a fluid situation with new revelations daily. Lenders need all the help they can get and an agent who understands is like an oasis in the desert.

Help your lender help you. When you are told that the lender needs 35 days, don't write a contract for a 25-day close. When you are told not to call daily for updates, because your lender just lost her best assistant and she is doing all she can, back off and send e-mails that can be addressed late in the day.

The one thing you want from a lender as a super agent is a timely close. Closing a transaction is the culmination of a long and arduous effort by many people and when a lender says they can't close timely, all that goodwill, all that elation, all that excitement, all that appreciation of your efforts withers and dies like unpicked fruit rotting in the sun. Your client is upset, the other agent is upset, and their client is upset. The erosion is faster than hurricane Sandy hitting the New Jersey coast and you are left with trying to assess damage and pick up the pieces. Do not let this reoccur. Know your lenders in the market.

Vendors

A vendor is anyone who provides a product or service during a transaction and a super agent makes it her business to know them all. Unlike the escrow officer or lender who may or may not be your recommendation, vendors serving your clients almost always come from you. You are the source of the source and your influence can and should be very powerful. Be sure that your vendors are qualified, courteous, on time, reasonable, alert, and responsive to your client's needs.

Your vendors are only as good as you make them. Make them accountable. Make them sensitive. Make them yours and in the process they will make your life better. Make them super vendors because the same five super powers you possess as super agents can and should belong to your vendors.

Your vendors should have the super power of putting the client first. Your roofer must be honest. Your plumber must be competent. Your home-warranty company must care and do the right thing.

Your vendors must be super communicators. Your electrician must be responsive and get back to you. Your heating, ventilation, and air-conditioning people must be able to articulate the problem to you and your client. Your septic and termite inspectors must turn in their reports timely.

Your vendors must be super motivators. Your painter must be able to ask questions to help you and your client get to where they know what they want. Your pool remodeler must be a good listener and your landscaper must draw their energy from giving clients what they want.

Your vendors must be super professionals. Your cleaning people must be trustworthy and know what chemicals to use and not use. Your window washer must have the proper equipment to get to hard-to-reach places and your floor person must protect the furniture during the installation process.

Finally your vendors must be super accountable. Your tradesmen must provide your clients with clear and accurate invoices and receipts. Your garage-door repairman must be able to tell you quickly when they replaced that pulley and all your vendors must keep their costs in line so that they provide your clients with parts and services at a fair and reasonable price.

Loyalty

What do you owe your allies, affiliates, and vendors? What do they owe you? Loyalty built on trust is the only loyalty that works. You must be able to rely on what you are told and your corporate family must know that what you say is true. Trust in business is a zero-tolerance game. Sure, people make mistakes. You will make mistakes. But you must own up to those errors and be prepared to make things right. You must expect this of yourself and you must expect it of others.

We used to write contracts by hand. We would fill in the blanks with our best printing possible but occasionally there was a mistake and usually it could be corrected with a cross out and everybody's initials. But one time we all missed a seven that looked like a nine and it made a $20,000 difference. Our seller thought this counter said $299,000 and so did we. The problem was that the buyer and buyer's agent thought they were offering $279,000 and when we accepted, they were thrilled. The error surfaced 30 days later, two days before closing, and the question of what to do became complicated. The first possibility was to cancel the whole deal. After all, the reasoning goes, there was no meeting of the minds. The buyer and seller were never actually in agreement. But the lender had done the loan. The title company had done the escrow. Money had been spent on the inspection and the appraisal. Repairs had been completed with the understanding that the vendors would be paid out of the closing distributions. Whose fault was this anyway? Was it the buyer's agent whose 7 looked like a 9 or ours for reading it wrong? Conveniently, at 6 percent, there was almost enough commission to cover it all. What did we do?

We paid the other agent her 3 percent and took the hit. It was the right thing to do. Over the years our title company has paid us back. Just look at what Alison did for our client when she took on the bank. That lender never forgot and has sent us business. Our client has brought us family members to serve. The other agent certainly never forgot. We did the right thing and because we did we can hold our vendors to the same standards.

You Cannot Succeed Alone

If you are that jerk from somewhere on the Pacific Coast and think you can succeed in a vacuum, get over it. You need people. You need everyone you can get. You need the agent community for if you break trust with them they will ruin you. You need strong affiliate relationships for they will have your back when you need them. You need great vendors because their good work will be a reflection on your recommendation. You need a corporate family that can depend on you and that you can depend on in return.

Put your clients first, serve them, and they will sing your praises in return. But, remember, clients are not the only ones talking about you. Make sure the words are kind.

Also remember that life is a two-way street and take the time to praise those who help you along the way. If you have a great lender, say so. If your escrow officer is a jewel, tell the world. No one succeeds alone. You cannot succeed alone.

You can do this.

Chapter 18 Summary

Other Agents

- We need each other.
- Treat with respect.
- Be a haven.
- Representation is not argumentation.
- Be courteous.

Title and Escrow

- Do not abdicate your role.
- Do not create flawed contracts.
- Accept their assistance.

Affiliate Power

- We can't always fix things.
- They have resources.
- Create a strong relationship.

Your Preferred Lender

- Lenders have a difficult role.
- Help your lender help you.
- A timely close is everything.

Vendors

- Only as good as you make them.
- Make them accountable.
- They should also have the five super powers.

Loyalty

- First, you must be loyal.
- You must be able to rely on others.
- You must be willing to do the right thing.

You Cannot Succeed Alone

- You need people.
- You need a corporate family you can depend on.
- Make sure their words about you are kind words.

19 Getting Help

Our industry is filled with wonderful agents who go it alone. We had one come to see us just the other day. Her name is Bobbie and she was one of the first agents we did a cross sale with 16 years ago. She had won a door prize for coming to see our listing on the luxury tour. We held the drawing afterward and then called the winners to come by our office for their gift.

JoAnn sat down with Bobbie to reminisce and Bobbie said she had been in real estate for 36 years. She was so happy for our success. We've done several deals with Bobbie over the years. JoAnn talked with her for about 10 minutes and then she was gone.

Afterward, we talked about what a sweet lady she is and how she had not changed a bit, which is a good thing because her clients are fortunate to have her. She is the consummate agent, puts her clients first, is honest, competent, and caring. She is a communicator, a motivator, a professional, and keeps good books. But Bobbie does it all herself. She has done it all herself for 36 years and she is happy but she makes about the same income, adjusted for inflation, as she did more than 30 years ago because there is simply a limit to what one person can do in a 24-hour day.

Unlikely to Change

We believe Bobbie likes it that way. She is comfortable doing everything. Of course, she has a strong relationship with her broker, other agents, and her affiliates but when it comes to licking stamps for a mailing, she likes to do it herself. The only other explanation would be that Bobbie fears the expense of hiring help. But that's not Bobbie.

Then we have Homer. He does it all himself because he is afraid of the expense. Homer worries that if he hires help, he may not make any more money than he does now and will end up with less. Homer has a scarcity mentality rather than an abundance mentality and Homer is unlikely to change.

What does not occur to either Bobbie or Homer is the possibility that having some help, even if it were a break-even or losing proposition, might buy them a little time to enjoy all that life has to offer. It also does not occur to them that extra time could lead to more business and to more of the satisfying part of being a real estate agent—serving clients and helping people.

You Are an Assistant

Let's face it. Someone less talented and less busy than you can perform much of what a real estate agent does. A super agent realizes this and knows that if you don't have an assistant, you are an assistant.

When JoAnn and I had been agents six months, we had three assistants and were making more money, after expenses, than any other time in our lives. We used the time we bought to make more deals and those deals led to more deals and super agency was born.

Over the years our team has grown to more than 30 licensed assistants (we go into detail with what they do today in Chapter 22), but it was a long growth process and we learned much along the way. Suffice it to say, we were not perfect delegators when we started but we did hit it lucky in some ways.

Don't Call an Assistant an Assistant

One of the things we never did was call an assistant an assistant. Not that we are all caught up it titles, we aren't, but we gave our people responsibilities and included those responsibilities in their job description. We have a transaction coordinator rather than a closing assistant. Assistants just don't have to be accountable. They are only there to assist. A coordinator, on the other hand, is expected to perform, to coordinate. We have showing agents, listing coordinators, and contract agents. But we have no assistants.

Let me tell you about Javier. He is a member of one of our mastermind groups and we've seen Javier over a luncheon meeting every month for almost 10 years. Javier is a rock star. Javier lists and sells property with the best. Javier makes well over a quarter million dollars a year and for as long as we've known Javier, he has been miserable.

Every month Javier's tale has been one of feast and famine. Javier would get ten homes in escrow and become so burdened with getting them through escrow he would fail to generate new leads and his business would slump after he got them closed until he could rebuild momentum. Javier knew this was his problem and he asked the group regularly for advice. We advised he hire help.

This led to the trail of assistants who did not work out. One month Javier would come to mastermind with talk of hiring an assistant and a few months later we heard about how it didn't work out. We worked through Javier's delegation skills and found that yes, he was not patient, but no, his assistants were not abused. The fact was that an assistant to Javier was a burden, someone he had to keep busy. The drama continued for years.

Then one luncheon, a member of the group stood up and said, "You're absolutely right, Javier. You don't need an assistant." Javier seemed relieved, as did several other members of the mastermind. Who needed the aggravation? We would just let Javier go on and suffer so that we didn't have to listen to it anymore. Then our fellow member continued, "You need a manager."

It was as if the earth moved. All this time we had been calling an assistant an assistant and burdening Javier with our mistake. Of course Javier did not need an assistant. He was a rock star. He needed a manager. Elvis needed the Colonel. Rocky needed Mickey Goldmill and Javier needed a manager.

We all joined in and Javier saw the light. Two months later Javier reported he had found a manager. Three months later he thanked the group in a way that embarrassed many and made a few of us tear up. Today, Javier has a manager and he is a rock star with time to enjoy his status. Javier is a super agent.

Simple Mission Statements

Another thing we did right is a clear description of duties and responsibilities. We created simple mission statements that work to this day. Marta was our first marketing director and we told her that her job was to create a steady stream of buyers and sellers. Donna was our first showing agent and we simply said bring them to the table. Donna's job wasn't to assist clients in finding their dream home. It was to bring the clients to the table ready to make an offer. Of course, Donna had to listen to the client and understand what they wanted and find them the home and show it to them. Sometimes she and they had to kiss a lot of frogs before they found their dream home, but she understood her mission in five words: bring them to the table. Marta had to do a lot of things, and wear a lot of hats to create a steady stream of buyers and sellers, but her eight-word mission statement kept her eye on the prize.

Systems

Our first owner broker explained once that the best response in a dispute resolution is, "This is how we always do it."

If you always do things the same way, it doesn't matter what it is, if you always do it the same way, you are bulletproof. All the miseries in real estate come from the explanation that in this particular circumstance, we did this or that. If you always meet the appraiser with comps, no one can say you unduly influenced their appraised value. If you always write in the same termite language on a contract, no one can say you did theirs differently and that's why the porch fell down. The porch may have still been destroyed but it is not your fault.

Systems keep everything you do the same. When do you create a system? Any time you find yourself doing something more than once, create a system for it. And when you create the system, document it. Reduce it to paper. Call it an instruction sheet, a tutorial, or procedure. Post it on a wall or put it in a binder. Keep a master list of all your systems and review them at least once a year. You will sleep better for it.

Think about this. If you are trying to do everything by yourself, what are the odds that you will always do things the same way? Let's face it. You are human and as such you are not programmed to be consistent. Yes, you can form habits but in real estate things evolve and if you have no one to bounce things off of, if you have no system to be accountable to, those changes occur gradually until you are not doing everything the same way.

Delegate It

We have heard a number of explanations for when to delegate. Here is our favorite. Any time you cannot affect the outcome, delegate it.

Think about your ability to affect the outcome. If you are scheduling a termite inspector, does it make a difference if you do it or someone else does? Are you going to affect the outcome? If you are inputting a listing on the Multiple Listing Service, are you going to affect the outcome? Yes, you may make a difference by going over the details and you may write a better description, but when it comes to sitting at a keyboard and punching in the data, you are really not going to affect the outcome. Are you really the right person to maintain your filing systems, to update spreadsheets, to input customer records on your CRM software? With all these tasks, you are not going to affect the outcome and you should give the job to someone else.

What should you delegate? Everything.

Delegate all the things you don't want to do. The first time we put a home in escrow, we attended the home inspection. It took two hours out of our day and the other agent told us their life story. At the end, our client showed up for a 10-minute verbal review by the inspector and we all left. That was our last inspection. We have team members do this and they probably do it better than us, especially when the process runs four hours on a small condo.

Delegate all the things you shouldn't be doing. That same escrow was about to close and we attended the final walk-through. We needed the money so badly back then, I felt the weight of the world at the prospect that some issue might come up and ruin the deal at the twelfth hour. I was too attached to the outcome and had no business being there. Today, we send Stuart or Chuck and I don't spoil my lunch.

Delegate all the things you cannot do. JoAnn is like Jekyll and Hyde. One minute she is the model businesswoman saying no to one unnecessary expense after the other and the next minute she is saying yes to the craziest request because she has a heart of gold. Those occasions are simple for someone else to resolve.

When you have help, you can delegate everything.

Don't Give It Away

The key to delegation is to not give it away. "Wait a minute," you say. "You just told me to delegate and now you say not to give it away?" That's right. If you delegate something and then wash your hands of it like Pontius Pilate, it will surely evolve away from whatever it was and potentially turn into your worst nightmare. The key is to create accountability. If you delegate the creation of comps for the appraiser, be sure you require that they be brought to you for approval before they go to that appraiser who can make or break a deal by coming in at value or not.

In time your review may become unnecessary, but only after your delegation has become a system, the review process has become redundant, and the help is doing whatever it is better than you ever did.

Reports

Ultimately the review process and the creation of systems becomes a report. Absent a summary of what is happening, all you have is data. You must have reports to know that systems are working and being worked. We have reports for everything and they all are delegated to the right person and they all have regular due dates. As a consequence, our office operates with little supervision and everyone knows what they are doing.

Be sure to stay in control by regularly reviewing reports. Just as your people have a regular time a report is due you must set and adhere to a schedule for reviewing them. Read your reports carefully with an eye to finding errors. One of the best things you can do for your team is to find an error and get back to the person who created the report. A small correction now and then keeps everybody on their toes.

Getting there is a thousand small decisions but first you have to make the decision to get help.

Super agents get help. You can do this.

Chapter 19 Summary

Unlikely to Change

- Some solo agents are just happy.
- Some solo agents are afraid.
- Neither considers the possibilities of getting help.

You Are an Assistant

- Others can do the work.
- Make more money after expenses.
- You are free to do what you do best.

Don't Call an Assistant an Assistant

- Assistants feel no responsibility.
- Javier felt an assistant was a burden.
- Javier needed a manager.

Simple Mission Statements

- Keep them clear.
- Keep them short.
- Keep them focused.

Systems

- Always do things the same way.
- If you do it a second time, create a system.
- Document everything you do.

Delegate It

- If you can't affect the outcome, delegate it.
- Delegate all the things you do not want to do, should not do, or cannot do.
- Delegate everything.

Don't Give It Away

- Don't wash your hands of what you delegate.
- Ask that things be brought to you for your review.
- Continue to review until no longer necessary.

Reports

- Reports confirm that systems are working and being worked.
- Delegate the preparation of reports.
- Review reports regularly and report errors back to the creator.

20 Partnering with Another Agent

When I was 12, an uncle of mine told our family about how he was cheated by a partner in an ice-cream truck business and I thought I would never want to be cheated like that. Going through high school it was as if I had an ear for failed partnerships and cheated partners. I would hear about how one partner ended up doing all the work in a business while the other collected his undeserved share and I would nod in agreement with my opinion reinforced over my uncle's misfortune. Our local grocer would refer to his silent partner and, because he was a somber man, I related his sadness to having a partner who contributed little because she didn't talk.

I had a best friend who studied accounting, and he spoke of partnership returns being a huge headache and how everybody needed to incorporate. I hate headaches, so I sure didn't want to ever be in a partnership.

It sounds so naïve now, but these are the kinds of misgivings and beliefs people grow up with. Perhaps you, too, have a funny feeling about sharing half of what you make with another person.

Marriage

Then I married JoAnn. I did it in a heartbeat and said the vows and never gave it a second's thought that I had now entered into the greatest partnership of all. We endowed each other with all our worldly possessions, which seemed easy because we didn't have much. But we had dreams and they were shared and they were priceless and we loved each other and I never once thought of my cheated uncle or my accountant friend. Marriage, however, is much different than a business partnership. Or, so it seems.

In a marriage you have love. In a business partnership you probably should at least like each other but, just as there are marriages of convenience, love and liking aren't absolutely required. More important would be a mutual respect for the other's skills, talent, and contribution. A partnership should be about filling gaps in each other. One partner's strengths complement the other partner's weaknesses. Without this fulfillment of each other's needs, two partners would simply be doubling up and creating no more than twice their individual contribution. A successful partnership should create more so that when the fruits of labor are evenly divided, each partner is getting more than they could have individually earned.

Marriage is for life, until death do us part, or we would certainly hope so but divorces do occur. Marriage is through sickness and in health. Isn't that one of the great attractions of a partnership? Knowing someone has your back and you have theirs is a wonderful security. Just taking a day off in a 24/7 business, which most service businesses are, is a big plus. Marriage procreates children. Partnerships create accomplishments, clients, and assets. Maybe marriage isn't much different than a business partnership after all.

Married couples who partner together in business are creating something more than a simple partnership. It is like a partnership within a partnership or a super partnership with its own unique set of challenges. Any time you add family emotions to business judgments you have challenges. JoAnn and I love being together. We share the load and enjoy each day, but most couples are unique and working together in a business partnership is the last thing they want to do. We know a couple who share a business and she says it's like dog years: every one equals seven. Married couples in business probably do not think about these things. They are married and they are in business and that's just the way it is.

The vast majority of super agents, however, are not married partners. Many are married. A number of them are married to a licensed spouse but they do not work together. Given a choice between a happy marriage and a successful business, always go for marital bliss and you can always find success on your own.

Partnership Plusses

So why would a super agent working alone partner up? As we've discussed, a heavy workload can be relieved with hiring help. Time is for sale. So buy it. For you, that might be just the ticket. As we have already stated, it makes no sense to combine your efforts with a partner only to achieve twice the results and then divide it in half and find yourself right back where you started. Let's look at all the partnership plusses.

1. **Two heads can be better than one.** In a super agent partnership, each of you is the other's coach, critic, and number one fan. With the right partner, creative juices flow. If you are operating alone you make decisions in a vacuum. As partners you can bounce ideas off each other. This is invaluable when it comes to lead generation. A single agent can grow into a box, doing the same things over and over, while two agents can help each other think outside the box to find new and better ways to get clients.

    Partners tend to identify problems quicker. Four eyes and four ears are better than two and two. It is easier to be super accountable when you have someone keeping you on track. Just showing up is more likely when you have a partner expecting you. Super communication is more likely when there are two agents concerned that every client got called back.

    Each of you is the other's key hire. If you have assistants or build a team (which we discuss in Chapter 21), finding key people will be your challenge and, with a partner, you already have your first one. Every business needs people at the top who can see what is needed and get things done. A partnership can provide twice the leadership.

2. **Having a partner gives you someone to share the peaks and valleys.** When things go wrong you have mutual support. Real estate sales, especially in residential resale, can be a very emotional environment. As much as you try to remain detached from the outcome, as much as you try not to feed the clients emotionality back to them, the process takes a toll on you personally and if you are alone with this stress, it can lead you to despair and burn-out. Having a partner to share this overload with helps you shed yourself of these burdens.

    When things go well you have someone to share the moment. Joy alone can have its own brand of sadness. It's like the merger party where the CEO is cashing in and she cannot understand why all the soon-to-be-fired executives aren't happy for her. In a partnership at least one other person is truly happy for you.

3. **A partnership provides perspective.** With a partner you have an opportunity to see yourself as others see you. Self-deception can be a subtle sickness. When a

mirror is your only reflection you tend to see what you wish. You don't age. You don't change. You don't have perspective. A partner gives it to you straight. At least they should. Be sure you are honest with each other. Mutual deception is just as bad if not worse than self-deception. When your super motivation stumbles and you fail to ask the right questions, your partner can see this happening and help you get on track. You can do the same for your partner. You are mutual safety nets and sentinels guarding against arrogance.

4. **You fill each other's gaps.** We don't all have the same strengths. We don't all learn at the same speed. We don't all acquire the five super powers at the same rate. A partnership reflects whichever partner is stronger or farther along. You get there quicker.

We also don't all have the same weaknesses and a partnership gives you an opportunity to ignore yours instead of trying to fix them. If you are a poor communicator and your partner is a super communicator, you can mutually agree to rely on her communication skills without having to immediately fix yours. This doesn't mean you shouldn't work on this super power, but you don't have to right away. Also, having a partner with a strength where you have a weakness gives you a model to emulate.

5. **Partners have twice the memory power.** Agents who work in pairs have the advantage of seeing and remembering details more accurately. They are each the others witness of what was said. JoAnn and I have total recall not only because we have good memories but also because we have each other to keep straight. I can't tell you how many times one of us has remembered something incorrectly or incompletely only to have the other provide corrections and details.

6. **Two people can present a solid front.** People might gang up on an individual but the dynamic completely changes when it is two on one or two on two. This is just human nature. You can overcome this on a listing appointment or when writing a contract simply by having an assistant present, but having a partner sitting next to you adds importance to the exchange.

When JoAnn and I sit down to list a home, she will do most of the talking while I observe the clients and attempt to perceive their needs and issues so that I can step in and cover something JoAnn may be missing. This gives JoAnn a moment to gather her thoughts and observe. This almost becomes a super power in itself—super understanding. It is seldom that a client ever lists with another agent after receiving the care that JoAnn and I provide as a solid front.

7. **Two people are more credible.** How would you like to have your own built-in praise person, someone who can say nice things about you at just the right time, every time? Partners do this all the time. You are talking to a client and you give your partner a big buildup. You are working with an affiliate or a vendor and your partner's timely praise seals the deal. Each partner is the other's best recommendation.

8. **Partners can be in two places at once.** How many times have you had to choose between two activities, functions or appointments? Now you can cover both. This is where partnerships were made for real estate. Just imagine reducing by half all those times you have to rearrange or reschedule.

   What about all that power of being together, a solid front and so forth? Not all clients are inflexible but some want attention and they want it now. At least on those occasions when you have two stubborn clients, you have an extra option that you don't have when going solo.

9. **You have an opportunity to be part of something greater than yourself.** Let's go back to that familiar refrain. Why would you want to give away half of what you make with no guarantee that you can double your income? You might want to go back a page or two and reread plusses one through eight. These are not business doublers. They are business exploders.

   Synergy is when one plus one equals three and that is what occurs when two super agents partner up. The result is much greater than simply doubling of the business. I suppose if two partners were to ignore all the advantages available and were to simply sit side by side in a shared office and each work their own book of business, they might simply combine incomes but a true partnership, well chosen and properly exploited, can easily exceed the combined separate incomes earned before. How much more? Considering all the variables, and this is pure conjecture on our part, we believe you can easily increase your earnings by half or more in a partnership. A great pairing can achieve unlimited success.

10. **You have each other's back.** In a partnership time becomes more manageable. You can take a day off. You can have a vacation. Catastrophic events can be handled. Imagine the security you would feel if you had an injury in an automobile accident

or contracted an illness and knew your clients would be taken care of and your business would not falter. We know an agent who doesn't register to vote for fear she might get jury duty and her business, in her mind, would collapse. Can you imagine giving up one of our more precious gifts as Americans simply because you have no one to watch your back?

This list is not complete because for many individuals the reasons and advantages of a partnership may be unique to them. It may accommodate a handicap or fix a family situation. Partnerships can have any number of reasons to exist.

Partnership Power

When Steve Wozniak was 21 he showed 16-year-old Steve Jobs a computer he had built. Wozniak only saw all the neat things the device could do and Jobs became consumed with marketing those neat tricks. Because of their partnership and mixing of talents we have iPhones and iPads today. Apple's stock valuation is the biggest of the big and it continues to grow because two guys got together and joined their strengths.

In 1975 Paul Allen combined the words microcomputer and software to create Microsoft. His partner, Bill Gates, had a vision of their putting their software on every desk in America. Together, they have far exceeded that goal as their products permeate our lives.

An introverted, map-making Meriwether Lewis needed the gregarious leadership of William Clark. These two very different individuals opened America's eyes to a sea-to-shining-sea union never imagined before.

Not all partnerships go on to great heights but they can be the spark to ignite a fire. Dean Martin, an Italian crooner, and Jerry Lewis, a wacky comedian, each went on to stellar careers but only after breaking into Hollywood as a partnership.

For some, the partnership launches one member over the other. Ike and Tina Turner, Sonny and Cher, and the Beatles come to mind. What are the odds of Tina Turner, Cher, and Paul McCartney achieving what each did without that springboard?

Many wondered why Hillary didn't divorce Bill and only those two individuals know for sure, but it is not a leap to believe that their partnership was a powerful glue that held them together, as well as a solid front that overcame a scandal that most forget while the masses remember the accomplishments of each.

Famous partners can come from family relationships. Wilbur and Orville Wright gave us flight. The Righteous Brothers gave us soul and inspiration. The Andrews Sisters redefined harmony, while George and Ira Gershwin gave us timeless melodies.

The list of famous pairings goes on and on: Hewlett and Packard, Gilbert and Sullivan, Smith and Wesson, Simon and Schuster, Sears and Roebuck, Procter and Gamble, Johnson and Johnson, Currier and Ives, Black and Decker, Barnes and Noble, Ben and Jerry, Abercrombie and Fitch. Their stories are fascinating in that they were opposites or colleagues, or they had so much in common. But in all of these, the combination created something greater than the parts.

If you are not yet sold on a partnership it may not be for you. But if you think partnering can get you where you want to go, let's look at what we need to do.

Written Agreement

Some of the greatest partnerships were started on a handshake but it is always best to document a partnership in the form of a written agreement. Beware of the standard or one-size-fits-all version of a partnership agreement offered by accountants and Internet sites. Before you draft an agreement you will want to sit down with your potential partner and hammer out the details. You need to ask the difficult questions. Most of these start with how do you want to handle this or what if that. Take your time in this process. Do this over several sessions so that you have time to reflect and see how it grows on you.

When you both feel comfortable, engage an attorney because legal minds work differently than yours and mine. Attorneys think about death, legacy, valuation, and taxes. A good attorney is always worth far more than their fee. You may want to consider a trial period before committing assets fully to your partnership. An attorney can advise you of your options.

Strengths and Weaknesses

One of the best reasons for a partnership is for each party to gain strengths of the other that are lacking in them. There are many real estate agents who are incomplete. They are great analyzers of contract terms but they have difficulty explaining or selling people on those term's merits. Others are great explainers who miss details. JoAnn is a much stronger people person than I am and I create spreadsheets that she could never conceive. When it comes to facing difficulties we seem to fall into a natural division and we rescue each other every day.

List your strengths and weaknesses. Use two columns or two sheets of paper but write them down. Have your potential partner do the same. Do these independently and then share the results with each other. Be honest with yourself and be honest with your partner. This process in and of itself will reveal much about your compatibility. If you cannot have an honest discussion about these personal issues then what happens when your business faces its first crisis?

You are looking for a partner who fills holes, who completes you. If you are both strong in one area, that may be a plus but if you are both weak in the same thing, now is the time to talk about it. This is not necessarily a reason to give up the relationship but you should both understand what you need do to overcome any deficiencies.

Division of Labor

Once you understand each other and know how to play to your relative strengths, you want to have a clear understanding of who does what. You don't need to get mired in minutia and detail here. You want to think in terms of responsibilities. In a partnership you will be relieving yourself of things that you will look to your partner to take care of and your partner will be doing the same. Make sure you both understand your mutual expectations of each other.

Realize that things change all the time in a business and that challenges you cannot begin to predict will rise up in the future. You should talk about this now. How will you handle a changing market? How will you make future decisions? Who can overrule and who can veto? Think about all these issues beforehand if you want to create a great partnership.

Dissolution

Not to put a damper on things but not all partnerships work out. Some partnerships may evolve into something unintended or unforeseen. The death of one partner may not end the partnership if the heir is willing, compatible, and capable but on the other hand you may come to find yourself wanting to go another direction. Address this up front. Put it on the table and come to an agreement beforehand.

One or both of you may want an exit strategy spelled out. An investor we know says he never invests a penny without knowing how he is getting his money back and what his sale price is. You may set a date for certain accomplishments. You may set a goal of incorporation or selling at a certain point. If you see eye to eye on these things up front you will eliminate future frustrations.

As we mentioned before, while not all partnerships last, they can be a springboard to success. Two people may very well begin with this end in mind.

Not all planning should be about potential problems and consequences. These should be addressed to be sure, but you also want to talk about what the partnership can do that you cannot do alone. Let your dreams soar. Create the vision and unleash the power of partnership.

You can do this.

Chapter 20 Summary

Marriage

- The greatest partnership of all.
- Similar to a business partnership in almost every respect.
- Not all married agents are partners.

Partnership Plusses

- Two heads can be better than one.
- Having a partner gives you someone to share the peaks and valleys.
- A partnership provides perspective.
- You fill each other's gaps.
- Partners have twice the memory power.
- Two people can present a solid front.
- Two people are more credible.
- Partners can be in two places at once.
- You have an opportunity to be part of something greater than yourself.
- You have each other's back.

(continued)

(*continued*)

Partnership Power

- Many partnerships are famous.
- Some partnerships launched solo success.
- Many famous partners were family first.

Written Agreement

- Hammer out the details.
- Ask the difficult questions.
- Engage an attorney.

Strengths and Weaknesses

- Many agents are incomplete.
- Both of you should list your strengths and weaknesses.
- Look for ways to fill holes and complete each other.

Division of Labor

- Have a clear understanding of who does what.
- Think in terms of responsibilities.
- Things change all the time in a business.

Dissolution

- Not all partnerships work out.
- Have an exit strategy.
- But focus on success.

21 Teaming Up

Real estate was a solitary profession at the beginning of the 1990s. An agent had their broker and affiliates, to be sure, and there were married couples and some family operations, but the vast majority of agents worked alone. We remember shortly after being licensed, hearing a lady speak at our broker's office meeting about providing transaction coordination services on a freelance basis and after she left many of the old crones talked about how that would never happen, paying out part of their commission for something they could do themselves. Change comes slowly.

JoAnn and I were innovators. When we began it seemed like everything we did was the opposite of what were the "how we do things because that's how we've always done things" accepted business practices. Our broker called one day and asked what a coming-soon sign was. Someone had obviously raised the question on our behalf.

I told Jim that we often had sellers whose home was not ready to show. Now, we had always gotten seller instructions to hold off on the MLS input until they were ready because the MLS rules are clear about putting listings on the system promptly, unless instructed otherwise, but we had also held off on putting up a sign as this was the current convention. Then, a lightbulb went on and we created the coming-soon rider. The logic was that we could build anticipation, take names of callers, and promise early notification just as the home went on the market. It was a no-brainer that had apparently not previously found a brain to enter. Today, coming-soon signs are everywhere.

We don't know who dreamed up the idea of a team approach to real estate agency, but when we came up with our own version of the concept it was a foreign idea in our market. A team is loosely defined as two or more agents branding themselves as a group or team. From there the definitions expand to the point that a team is what an agent or group of agents says it is.

Brokers Employ Agents

This might be a good time to clarify the difference between an agent and a broker. An agent works directly with clients in the name of and with the oversight of a broker. A broker employs agents and authorizes them to do business. All contracts are executed in the name of the broker. Escrows belong to the broker. Listings belong to the broker. Brokers typically hire and fire agents, provide training and office space, resolve disputes between agents, and settle complaints by clients. Brokers seldom handle a transaction directly with and for a client and when they do, it is fair to say for our purposes here that they are acting as an agent in those circumstances. Many agents go on to get their broker's license for added prestige but, at least in Arizona, they are called associate brokers working for a designated or employing broker and when working with a client, they are agents. In Colorado they did away with the agent license altogether but the remaining brokers are fulfilling the agent role when servicing clients.

This can all become rather confusing when an agent decides, as we did, to form their own brokerage. After a dozen years with our original broker, we were told that they were merging with another franchise and we would have to move all our licenses to this new brand. At the time JoAnn was our one agent and the rest of our team was listed as licensed assistants to JoAnn. Faced with changing all our signage and doing all the paperwork anyway, we decided to form our own brokerage. Other than creating a separate broker entity, designating our employing broker, and instituting broker-management procedures, nothing has really changed. Our brokerage has only one agent (and she is a lot of trouble) and the rest of us are licensed assistants to JoAnn. We are often referred to as a boutique brokerage because of our size.

Another kind of brokerage is the sole-proprietor broker, who wears all the hats at once. Even in this circumstance, when a sole-proprietor broker is working with a client, they are acting as an agent.

By the turn of the millennium, teaming up was in full swing and took many forms, a diversity that continues to this day. We will describe three basic team structures, their advantages, their challenges, the things they have in common, and the ways in which they are different. Bear in mind that every team is unique and there are thousands of variations. By breaking them into three types you will be able to recognize the different dynamics that create such a panorama of choices. This understanding can help you decide what kind of team you might wish to join or form.

A Simple Team

The simplest team is one in which several agents operate in the same space but each serves their own client list. The business can be reported individually or it can be credited to the agent who is in the leadership role. The team leader or owner is usually the founder or the one willing to underwrite the operation and guarantee the landlord's lease. The advantages of a simple team to the agents are shared administrative services like transaction coordination and a shared branding umbrella which expands their individual exposure to the combined exposure of all the agents' efforts.

The client's experience is unchanged from that of having a solo agent. All communication is routed through the one agent with whom the client has the relationship. The client may have the illusion of working with a larger entity but they are still reliant upon the one agent for all their key services.

The agent experience is one of having the security or support of a team but their actual day-to-day endeavors are unchanged from being a sole practitioner.

There are few shared systems or rules on a simple team. Most commission sharing is through referral agreements between the agents. By pooling resources—sharing costs such as utilities, or tracking individual costs such as copier use—expenses are usually covered. There are some economies of scale with subsequent cost savings to the individual agent. Many simple teams operate on a handshake while others put together a simple agreement for all team members to sign. Joining or leaving a simple team is not much different from switching brokers.

The advantages of a simple team are instant credibility, camaraderie, mentorship, and expanded lead generation through branding. A team may provide an agent with motivation that he or she might be unable to generate for themselves.

The disadvantage is that the responsibility to generate business remains with the individual; this sometimes leads to disappointment for agents who expected more from the team. Also, on a simple team any investment in branding is predominantly spent on the team and when an agent makes a change that investment is gone.

The greatest challenge of a simple team is matching agents for compatibility. For instance, a simple team with a mix of super agents and not-so-super agents may find difficulty finding a common attitude toward success. A team with all super agents or all less ambitious agents may find commonality and benefit more from working together.

A Rainmaker Team

A rainmaker team is built around the personality and lead-generation talents of one super agent or a partnership of super agents. This team or a variation thereof represents the vast majority of teams serving our industry today. On a rainmaker team the rainmaker is king. The rainmaker brings in the business, pays the expenses, creates the rules, and makes a profit or loses money depending on how well they operate as a business.

The client's experience is one of being assigned to a listing agent for all listing needs or being assigned to a buyer's agent for all their purchase needs. Other than this division of focus, the client remains dependent on a single agent to serve them through the purchase or sale of their home. If they are doing both, selling and then buying, they may have one agent taking care of them but more often two, each handling the sale side and the buy side respectively.

Rainmakers are predominantly listing agents with a large inventory bringing in buyer interest. A few rainmakers came up as buyer agents and have little or no interest in the listing side. They know how to generate buyer business far beyond what they can handle and they lead a team of buyer agents. In both instances, buyer's agents are generally given the buyer lead on a fifty-fifty split and expected to handle the transaction from there.

The buyer's agent experience on a rainmaker team can be very fruitful, provided the promised leads are produced and the quality of those leads is good. Relieved of the burden of lead generation, the buyer's agent can focus on the client and usually sells more than twice the number of homes than they would otherwise sell on their own. The problems come when the leads, or at least the perception of the leads, falter and the buyer agent is left without clients to show. Because markets cycle and because it is difficult for rainmakers to sometimes keep up the pace, turnover among buyer agents can be high.

Rainmakers generally are good businesspeople who rely on systems and rules to keep everything running smoothly. A rainmaker team is sometimes described as a benevolent dictatorship. Another analogy is "She who has the gold, makes the rules." So don't expect a vote if you are a member of a rainmaker team. You have hitched your wagon to a star and you want very much for that star to succeed.

Can a super agent survive and thrive on a rainmaker team? Certainly a future super agent can learn at the knee of a rainmaker. Rainmakers are proven super agents and having an opportunity to work closely with them is beyond measure. Often rainmakers are looking for an agent to buy or continue their business and a super agent might pay their dues for such an opportunity. Sometimes super agents grow into a partnership with a rainmaker as they hone their lead-generation skills. Certainly, if you are set on a solo career as a super agent, you should go for it, but exposure to a rainmaker can be life changing.

The advantages of a rainmaker team are instant financial security that you may find difficult to achieve on your own. The disadvantages are that the rainmaker overshadows the accomplishments of the individual.

The greatest challenge for a rainmaker, and therefore the team, is the constantly changing market. Markets swing from buyer markets to seller markets. Distress and inventory levels rise and fall. Financing gets tight or the money flows. These are the realities of real estate and generating a steady stream of buyers and sellers at a high level is not an easy task even for a rainmaker.

The Structured Team

A few rainmakers manage to elevate their business to a higher level in which they can move into the role of business owner with all responsibilities, including lead generation entirely delegated to the team. The rainmaker turned business owner can then focus entirely on the business rather than working in the business.

A structured team is organized with a CEO, the former rainmaker, and three divisions: listings, buyers, and administration. Each of these divisions are operated by a managing executive who is given responsibility for all aspects of their division. Lead generation remains a goal of all divisions. There is some debate about whether these division executives should be former super agents or trained executives capable of directing what amounts to a corporate structure. The easy answer is that they should be both but we think that it may be easier to teach the real estate component to an executive rather than trying to teach leadership to an agent whose only qualification is real estate success.

The listings division is divided into the acquisition of listings, managing the listing file, and negotiating offers.

The buyers or sales division is focused on the acquisition of buyers, showing property, and writing offers.

The administrative division is responsible for transaction coordination, lead generation, systems, accounting, and office management.

The client experience is similar to that of other teams or working with a solo agent, in that one agent takes them through the transaction, is their single point of contact, and is their impression of the team.

The agent experience on a structured team is one of clear rules, good systems, and strong support. A super agent wishing to specialize may find fulfillment here as well as learning what it takes to create their own structured team in the future. There is opportunity for advancement similar to climbing the corporate ladder.

The advantages of a structured team are a strong probability for long-term success because the CEO and executive managers are able to focus on long-range planning. A structured team is able to innovate and adapt to changing market conditions.

The disadvantages of a structured team can be the structure itself. There is limited opportunity for self-expression and for that reason alone it may be difficult to attract talent that would be otherwise available.

The greatest challenge for a structured team is the emphasis on proper recruitment. The three division leaders are the keys to success and a problem with any one of the three must be addressed immediately.

Is a Team for You?

There are thought leaders who say that teams are the face of the our profession's future and there are wise minds who say we will always have the individual or solo agent working hard to serve their limited number of clients. We think they are both correct. Teams are here to stay and so are solo agents. The balance between the two has yet to find equilibrium, but you are free to make your choice without fear of becoming obsolete or having to adapt to something unappealing to you later.

The greatest challenge for a solo super agent is time. Even with assistance there is a limit on how many clients you can ultimately serve. The solution for a solo agent who wants to do more becomes transition to a team. This natural progression to team creation is the most reliable because the super agent who outgrows a solo practice is one who has become a rainmaker.

The challenge for any team is making rain or creating more business. A team is always hungry because there are more mouths to feed. Any team formed in the absence of a rainmaker will have to address this deficiency or it will wither away for lack of leads. Any time saved without business to fill it is time wasted.

Is a team for you? Perhaps. If you are unable to manage time, a team gives you structure. If you are unable to motivate yourself, a team may give you direction. If you struggle with one or more of the super powers, a team may fill your gaps. But do not expect a team to solve all your problems or cover all your weaknesses. A team is not the answer to deeper issues. Teams need talented people who wish to work with other talented people toward a common goal.

Chapter 21 Summary

Brokers Employ Agents

- Brokers seldom work directly with clients.
- Brokers hire, fire, and resolve disputes.
- Agents serve clients.

A Simple Team

- Several agents—one brand.
- Each works own clients.
- Client experience is unchanged versus solo agent.
- Advantages—credibility, camaraderie, mentorship, and branding.
- Challenges—compatibility.

A Rainmaker Team

- Built around single personality—the super rainmaker.
- Not a democracy—rainmaker makes the rules.
- Client Experience—buyer agent and listing agent.
- Advantages—financial security.
- Challenges—dealing with market changes.

(continued)

(continued)

A Structured Team

- Organizational chart.
- CEO and three divisions—Listings, Buyers, Administrative.
- Client experience—same as rainmaker team.
- Advantages—long-term potential and opportunity to grow.
- Challenges—recruitment.

Is a Team for You?

- Both teams and solo agents are here to stay.
- Time-challenged solo agents can grow on a team.
- Team doesn't eliminate the need for talent.

22 The Super Team

"We've moved to Any City, USA and we want to know who does real estate here like you did when you sold our home." This a familiar phone call to us.

"My husband and I have sold 13 or 14 homes over our lifetimes and we have never had it handled this way before." We've heard a variant of this many times.

"My dad explained how you guys are different, so who do I see next?" This is a new client referral from an old client.

"Okay, JoAnn. You can stop calling me now." This was our favorite turnaround, a negotiator of defense contracts whose previous real estate agents, as he perceived them, did not communicate with him once the listing was signed.

Do Not Finish This Book

If you are satisfied so far, if you are a solo agent, happily partnered, or a member of a team as described up to now, if you are excited to implement all the super secrets and gain all the super powers described to this point, stop here and do not finish this book.

This may sound crazy. We just went through 21 chapters in which a super agent makes more money and does a better job for the client. But now we are going to talk about a different approach, a super team, and on a super team everything gets turned upside down and backwards. A super team is the answer to the reality of a changing market.

In Chapter 5, we talked about the fact that clients are empowered today. They have all the information. Empowered clients even have plenty of resources to interpret this information. These clients do not wish to be dependent upon their agent for information. These clients wish to be served at a higher level. These clients want super service and they want to be put first.

Traditional agents who rely on the dependent-client model—making proprietary information or the interpretation of that information their business bastion—will find themselves serving a smaller and smaller audience. A super team is predicated on the ideas of putting the client at the center of the transaction and gaining that client's loyalty through super service. This is a completely different offering and we believe it will be a growing part of our profession.

The Client Wheel

A super team approaches a real estate transaction from the client's viewpoint. Whether a client wishes to be empowered or remain dependent does not matter. Either way, a client's viewpoint and needs are the same. For example, a client thinks of selling and then buying. The first thing the client needs to know is if this is even feasible. How much will their home sell for? This tells them if they have equity and how much. How much will it cost to buy what they want? This tells them if it is worthwhile to make a change. In the case of a client who must move, the motivation becomes more urgent but these needs remain the same. They need answers and whether they get them through their own research or by asking an agent is their choice.

Once they have decided to sell, they need more answers and possibly advice. What do I need to do, if anything, to get the house ready? Who do I wish to employ to get the home sold? What do I have to do once the house is on the market? Buyer-clients ask: Where do I want to live? What is available? How do I see inside? Each of these questions is a step in the process and for each step their need for an agent may vary. In the traditional experience, a single agent tries to take care of all these client needs and tries to take care of numerous clients who are all at different points in their individual process.

A super team puts the client at the hub of a wheel and provides a specialized super agent at each spoke or client need. To get the home ready, the client needs an agent specialized in assessing the home's needs. To price the home, the client needs a prelist agent who specializes in market comparisons. To list the home, the client needs a counselor to explain the process. To prepare for marketing, a client needs an agent specialist to create marketing materials. Once on the market, the client needs a listing coordinator to manage showings. When an offer comes in, a client needs a contract specialist to advise and negotiate for them. Once sold, a client needs a transaction coordinator to take them from contract to close. A solo super agent may wear all these hats; on a super team each hat sits on a different head.

The result is a client wheel that rolls the client smoothly through the process.

All this does not happen without planning and there are challenges along the way. This is where things get upside down.

The Super Team

JoAnn and I have heard over and over that our client experience is unique because our super team is unique. In 16 years, we have not found anyone who operates in quite the same way we do. We are not saying that ours is the only way or even the best way to do business. We certainly don't have the market cornered on smarts. There are agents who do as much or more business than we do. But we do have a number of things we do differently and all over the country agents ask us constantly about our methods. We will attempt here to define our uniqueness and to tell you why we think ours is a great way to represent buyers and sellers of residential real estate.

The Client Experience

A client dealing with us for the first time may be surprised that we make no effort at client dependency. A dependent client is imprinted on a single agent to answer all their questions and provide all their services. Because we realize that the era of private or proprietary information is gone and the era of the empowered client has arrived, we put the client in charge. For some clients this is a radical shift and we have to explain or sell these clients on their newfound power. Returning clients already know how we operate differently and do not want to go back to the old way of doing things.

The difference begins with the first phone call. If you are a potential client, the first voice you hear is a licensed agent who is there to serve you. We do not employ an unlicensed receptionist to field calls, get your information, and have someone call you back. That model is the first step toward client dependency. Instead, the agent who answers your call simply wants to know what you need. There is no phone tree, no effort at prequalifying, only a desire to help. If this is your first call the answering agent quickly determines if you are buying, selling, or both, where you are in the process, and immediately transfers you to the right person to serve you.

If you are thinking of selling your home, the next voice you hear is the new-listings coordinator. Her job is to help you with answers to your questions and to ask you the right questions to quickly understand your situation and what you need. She collects your name, contact information, and property address and offers a listing appointment. If that is your desire, she then schedules an advance-team appointment and a listing appointment, explaining the purpose of each and selling the concept that you will be working with a series of agents who are experts and specialists at each step of the selling process.

The advance team appointment is an information-gathering effort. The AT agent delivers the prelist package, which has information about us and then goes through the home gathering all the details necessary to put the home on the market. He takes a series of file photos, measures all the rooms, gathers more information about why the seller is moving, and further sells the next step—the listing appointment.

The listing agent arrives for your appointment. She has already looked over the AT file but asks to briefly walk through the home to see for herself. Then she sits down with you to explain the listing process and answer any questions you may have. She provides market info, a price is established, you sign the papers, and she explains the steps from here. She explains that the listing coordinator will call to schedule several appointments. These will include the stager, the photographer, in some cases the cleaners, the videographer, the repair people when needed, and so on. You are told you will get a copy of the MLS to review for errors prior to going live on the market.

Once on the market you will get calls from any one of our agents to schedule either a showing by one of our agents or by an agent from another brokerage. You receive feedback after showings. You get called about ad insertions and you get asked if an open house is okay on a certain date. If your home isn't sold in 30 days, you get a call about showings to date, what we might do to encourage offers, and if a price adjustment is in order.

At this point you have talked to or worked with 5 to 10 different agents who you may or may not remember by name, but the important thing to you is that you are being heavily communicated with, your home is being marketed in the best way possible, and every time you call you are immediately served by a licensed agent who knows where you are in the process, answers your questions, and gets done what you want done. You are in charge.

Compare this to the dependent-client model where you must reach your agent for every detail. If your agent is busy with another client, you must wait for a call back. When you do get your agent on the phone you feel pressure to remember all your issues so you don't have to go through the whole process of getting your agent again. You feel dependent upon your agent and grateful for their time instead of the other way around. Now, there are many super agents out there who take their client calls or get back quickly. These super agents do a wonderful job and to be dependent upon them is not an imposition or a bad thing; but we are talking about the client experience here and being able to make a call and get it done beats waiting for a call back.

Does this mean we never have to call a client back? Of course not, but this kind of phone traffic is reduced by at least half and callbacks are handled quickly. No call is left unreturned at the end of each day.

Client Ownership

On our super team every client is referred to as a client of the firm. There is no client ownership by an individual agent because client ownership leads to client dependency and our goal is client empowerment. On a super team, each agent specializes on their step and they end up touching all the clients as they cross their desk. Every client is important to every agent and every team member feels a responsibility to the rest of the team to take care of every client. There is no room for client ownership.

As soon as you identify Mrs. Jackson as Mary's client, you have created client ownership. The minute Don thinks that the Carsons are his clients, you have opened the door to so many negative emotions. The smooth operation of a super team depends on teamwork and client ownership introduces greed, envy, arrogance, pettiness, and resentment. When agents think of clients as something to own that puts more money in their pocket, they want as many clients as they can get without regard to whether the client is best served: "Just give me more clients so I can make more money." Agents who see other agents owning clients that for whatever reason they cannot have, envy that successful agent. They become petty about perceived disparities and injustices and in the end resent each other. Office alliances are formed and the client is lost in the shuffle.

"What about competition?" you ask. Competition drives innovation. Competition stirs achievers to achieve more. You need competition in sales. Competition serves the consumer by driving down costs. All this is true but within a team, competition can be a disease. Competition has its place. The team can compete with other teams to succeed. The team can compete with itself to exceed its own expectations or the expectations of those it serves, but teammates must bond together in mutual reliance and support.

Cutting the Cord

Client dependency and client ownership are enough of a threat to client empowerment that on a super team we take specific steps to cut the cord whenever possible. Cutting the cord is an analogy to the moment an infant is separated from its mother as the doctor cuts the umbilical cord. Suddenly, the dependent baby is empowered. The child has free will. The mother's role changes from the giver of life to a lifetime of serving and protecting that child. To be sure, the child has needs and cannot make it on their own but once the cord is cut the child and mother are forever changed.

One of the places where we cut the cord is when a buyer wants to write an offer. Up to this moment, a client may have only dealt with one person on the team, the showing agent. Perhaps they met at an open house, or this agent helped them when they called for information on a property with a yard sign. They may even be past clients, returning for more good service.

Looking at homes can be a very bonding experience. The client and the showing agent look at homes on the computer. They e-mail back and forth. They ride together. They walk through homes and talk about likes and dislikes. By the time they have found the house, the client has built a lot of dependency in the showing agent. And it must end.

To continue this happy union is not in the client's best interest or the team's best interests. One of the reasons that everything has been such a smashing success up to now is that showing is all that a showing agent does on a super team. A super showing agent knows how to get the client where they want to be. They know all the right questions to motivate the client to come to a good decision and find not just *a* house but also the *right* house for them. A super showing agent knows the inventory—what just hit the market and what just fell out of escrow. A super showing agent knows all the listing agents and how to gain quick access. A super showing agent knows their job and knows their mission, which is to bring the client to the table ready to make an offer. Up to now the super showing agent is just what the client needs.

But let's say we don't stop there. We have the showing agent write the contract, which is another skill set entirely. Now, that showing agent who has developed all those good relationships with listing agents to get access is now the negotiator with that listing agent. The showing agent whose previous time challenge was juggling showings now has to juggle not only showing clients, but also clients who want to make offers or counteroffers.

Now, let's say we go further and have the showing agent, because they are the ones with the relationship with the client, and because the client is now imprinted and dependent upon that agent, meet the client at the house for the home inspection once they are in escrow. This takes more time away from showing and serving other clients who want to see houses.

Now that the showing agent completely owns the client and the transaction, let's just go ahead and have them conduct the final walk-through and closing.

No. We cut the cord and the client is better for it and we cut the cord so the showing agent can go back to showing other clients.

Selling the Handoff

Although it may change in the future as more and more super teams are formed, clients today do not naturally fall into the mindset of being handed off through the buying or selling process. Most clients have the traditional expectation of having one agent serve all their needs and must be initially sold on the new model. This is surprisingly easy and the payoff is client loyalty. Once clients have the super team experience they become fiercely loyal because they do not want to slip back into dependency. They want empowerment.

This change is accomplished by selling the handoff all the time. In the example of the showing agent showing property, clients will come up with questions that are better addressed later. Certainly every question is important and to put that client first you must answer them all and answer them fully. But clients often put the cart before the horse and their best interests lie in telling them so. We often describe real estate as a winding road with a series of bridges to be crossed. It is only human nature to look ahead but when the client is looking past their next bridge we must help them keep focused. And the focus is completing the next step.

Say for example the client who hasn't found the right home yet, asks about a seller's motivation. Why are they moving? This is a valid question about the home you love but not for every home you look at. When buyers get ahead of themselves, it is a distraction that is not in their best interests. This is an opportunity to sell the contract step.

The showing agent then describes to the buyer how, when the client has found the right home and wants to make an offer, they will sit down with the contract team and we will find out everything possible about the house. The contract agent will call the listing agent. We will pull the complete listing history and the tax record. We will do everything possible to understand the seller's motivation in order to craft a successful offer.

Even if you are a solo super agent this is a valid answer to keep a buyer focused, but in this instance—in a super team environment—it is an opportunity to sell the future. After two or three such questions by the buyer and answers by the showing agent, the client is motivated to find that house so they can move on to that promised next step.

Selling the handoff is something every member of the team does constantly because it is in the client's best interests, it keeps them on track through an otherwise confusing experience, and it puts them first.

The Agent Experience

Super agents on a super team have an opportunity to specialize and become incredibly good at what they do. A listing agent who lists 300 to 400 homes a year is much more able to sit down with a client and see what needs to be done, what pricing strategy is best, and what marketing will be most effective. The client is better served and the team can rely on a steady stream of buyers and sellers because listings attract buyers.

A contract agent who deals only with writing and negotiating a dozen or so offers each week is much more capable of getting it right every time. Making a deal is as much art as it is legalese and an agent who specializes in winning for the client will have a high rate of success.

A transaction agent who closes 30 to 40 files a month can keep every escrow on track because that is all she does. She can systematize the process and communicate on a schedule because that is all she does. As a consequence, the client who is in escrow is always apprised of what is happening and what comes next.

This specialization does not relieve the specialized agent of the need to have and exercise super powers. The super agent on a super team has an opportunity to practice their super powers at an elevated level.

The specialized agent has the power to put the client first. Because their role is defined and limited, within that scope the super team agent is totally empowered to put the client first. Honesty is an absolute. No team member can hope to make it up as they go. They know that this client will be continuing down the line, so total disclosure is the only path that works in this system. The agent as an individual and the team as a whole must trust the truth. The client is best served and the whole team sleeps well.

A super team agent must be competent. The whole team and the whole system depend on each agent knowing their job and doing it well. A super team creates far fewer issues that the broker ends up having to resolve. This puts the client first.

And a super team agent cannot be concerned with their personal situation. Everything they do must be about the client's needs. They must care about the client's dreams and goals. They draw their motivation from the stream of clients and they put them all first. Additionally, a super team agent puts his or her teammates first. She must be honest, competent, and care about the team's goals because to do otherwise would let the team down. A true team is bigger than any individual and on a super team the super power of putting the client first is magnified in its strength.

A specialized agent has the super power to motivate because they don't have to know every possible question to ask. They don't have to fix everything. They only have to know all the right questions to ask to help the client through this particular step. The client is put first. A specialized agent has the super power of professionalism because they are busy every day. It becomes rote that they inform and consult the client because it is always the client's decision.

The super team agent is super accountable. Because each step is intertwined, every super agent on a super team knows they must complete all their software entries, keep client records up to date, turn in their reports, and finish all the other details that make all the difference. Their teammates depend on it. As a result, a super team knows its numbers.

Super Team Advantages

- **A super team builds a following.** Every time a client is converted to being empowered rather than dependent, they are attached to the super team that converted them. This leads to super loyalty and a line of new clients related to past clients. The strength of this database feeds the super team in good times and bad.
- **A super team has very little turnover.** After 16 years we have 15 agents who have averaged 10 years with the team. New members learn quicker and those who do not fit stand out like a neon sign.
- **A super team has a huge potential.** When markets swing positive, the additional business does not necessarily dictate additional agents. When business tripled in 2005 we added only three people in assistant roles.

- **A super team can scale.** A super team can have as few as three agents, each wearing a number of hats while guarding against client ownership, empowering the client, selling the handoff, cutting the cord, and specializing in their roles. Growth is accommodated by divesting each team member of a hat or two as they give them to a new member. When the super team grows to more members than hats it is because of the business volume and some positions have to have several agents. Showing agents are a good example. A 30-member super team may require six showing agents to accommodate client needs.

- **A super team has downside protections.** While no business can survive unscathed in a market meltdown, a super team is largely unaffected by the expected dips and valleys. A super team with a database of loyal empowered clients benefits from the advocacy of those clients and market slowdowns are less impactful on the super team. In any market, there is always some business and the super team gets its share. A super team is the last to lose and the first to benefit.

- **Because of their volume, a super team is more sensitive to market conditions and better able to control costs.** Because a super team's lead generation is based on client advocacy, marketing costs can be minimized in slow markets and maximized in opportunity markets. Sales volume can be better stabilized and predictable. A super team is a bigger ship less affected by small waves.

Super Team Challenges

A super team is constantly tempted to grow. As the client database expands, there is pressure to expand the team. This is a good thing but finding and developing talented team players is not that easy. The agent landscape is littered with agents who celebrate client dependency and client ownership. They thrive on competition and are not about to change. There is nothing wrong with this. Many of these agents do a fine job but you are looking for agents able to go a different direction. A super team needs super teammates.

One solution is to grow your own and we have done this. We hired clients and sent them to school. We trained them to the super-team method and they wouldn't think of doing this on their own, us included. JoAnn wouldn't do this without me, I certainly wouldn't do it without her, and neither of us would do this without a team.

Over the years we have successfully hired experienced agents. Their expertise has been a welcome addition but their old habits have been a challenge. Not all of them have made it but those who did are our greatest advocates because they know how much greater the satisfaction is.

Our team dynamic is wonderful. The daily interaction is amazing. Observers find it difficult to understand. Even our affiliates and vendors puzzle over how well our systems work. But our clients rave over the experience. They move away and want to know who can serve them in their new city, like we did in Scottsdale. They marvel at how much better their experience is this time. They send family and friends, telling them they have to use us because it is so much better. They joke with us that we can stop calling them now because their communication experience was so good that they will never go elsewhere. And they come back again and again.

This is the super team as we have built it. You can build one, too.

Chapter 22 Summary

Do Not Finish This Book

- Everything turned upside down and backwards.
- Empowered clients want super service.
- A completely different offering.

The Client Wheel

- The client is at the hub.
- The spokes are the client's needs.
- Rolls the client through the process.

The Super Team

- Unique.
- A number of things different.
- A great way to represent buyers and sellers.

(continued)

(*continued*)

The Client Experience

- No effort at client dependency.
- Licensed agents—no unlicensed receptionist.
- An expert at each step.
- Client is in charge.
- Immediate help rather than callbacks.

Client Ownership

- Every client is a client of the firm.
- Eliminates greed, envy, arrogance, pettiness, and resentment.
- Competition within a team can be a disease.
- Super team competes for client.
- Mutual reliance and support.

Cutting the Cord

- The moment the doctor cuts the umbilical cord, the child is empowered.
- The moment the home is found, buyer-agent dependency must end.
- Dependency is not in the client's best interest.

Selling the Handoff

- Clients expect the traditional one-agent model.
- Each agent along the way sells the handoff.
- It eliminates confusion and puts the client first.

The Agent Experience

- Specializing creates opportunity to become incredibly good.
- Specialized agents still have and exercise the super powers.
- They put the client first. They are honest, competent, and care.
- They communicate and motivate.
- They are professional and accountable.

Super Team Advantages

- Low turnover.
- Upside potential.
- Can scale.
- Downside protections.
- Able to control costs.

Super Team Challenges

- Pressure to grow.
- Finding and developing talent is not easy.
- A super team needs super teammates.

23 A Super Life

Work

A super agent works less hours. A super agent knows that the answer to more money is not in working more. Fifty hours do not produce 25 percent more income than 40. Eighty hours a week does not double your income. It destroys your dreams, your ambition, and your health. Take time off. Schedule it. Arrange to take Sunday, Tuesday, or Wednesday and then start working on another day of the week. Recharge your batteries so you can enjoy the ride.

The goal, however, is not to eliminate working entirely. Those who do not work miss out on life's treasure, the reward of achievement and the satisfaction of accomplishment. Work only for these things and the money to pay for the rest. You must have a life outside your profession.

Family

Take care of your family relationships. Family is from cradle to grave. You are born a child and remain a child until all before you are gone. You become a spouse or life partner and if you are lucky they are there until the end. You become a parent and your children go on after you. Learn to forgive. Outside of your spouse, you don't get to pick family. Dysfunction is the order of the day and love must come first. Forgive, forget, and enjoy your super life.

Health

Take care of yourself. Only when we lose our health do we fully appreciate what a gift well-being can be. Happiness lives in a healthy body and despair lives in disease. Choose happiness and support that decision with good health. The number one killer is stress. It kills your joy and then it kills you. Do not risk more than you can lose. Be prepared for a no in order to get a yes. Have an outlet. Open your safety valve and let some air out. JoAnn and I celebrate Slug Saturday and Sunday becomes our best day of the week.

Appreciate your health and say thank you by watching what you eat, getting enough exercise, and thinking prevention. Get checkups. Take vitamins. Face illness as a challenge and seek early detection. We all have a limited time on Earth. Make it a healthy experience.

Wealth

Live within your means. Money troubles cause stress. If you destroy your financial security your health will suffer. There is nothing wrong with seeking riches. We all have bills to pay and money already spent but the poor rapidly dispose of every penny, often awaiting their next check with empty pockets. The wealthy release their money slowly and never let go of their last dollar. Wealth protects your well-being. Your first priority should be financial reserves. Live within your means and pay yourself first. Savings are what you keep before you spend because nothing is ever just left over.

Save all you can on your taxes. They are life's largest expense. But once your exemptions are exhausted, pay your taxes. When you think money troubles are the worst, tax troubles trump it all. Set aside what will ultimately belong to the government. To play with these funds is to play with fire.

Remember this: credit is permission to owe money. The concept of borrowing comes from business. Opportunities for future success can justify the expense of money now for more money later. But consumers often have no other justification for ransoming their future income than current pleasure. The purchase of a home justifies a mortgage because it is repaid with money that would otherwise go to rent. The purchase of a car on payments is only a way of spreading the cost over the time while you operate the vehicle. Borrowing for education now can return greater earnings in the future. Otherwise, live within your means.

Investment

Invest in what you know. If you work for a giant corporation, buy stock; if you work for the government, buy municipal bonds. If you are a super agent, buy real estate. For that matter everyone should buy real estate and you should be the one selling it to them, but you know your market. You have insider knowledge that the SEC can't knock on your door and arrest you for using.

Do you know the number one, surefire way to earn 5 percent more than the going rate on savings accounts and money markets? This method has no downside risk and is 100 percent guaranteed. Simply pay off your mortgage and when you don't owe money on your home, purchase and pay off another piece of property. Every time you reduce your mortgage by a hundred dollars, you have earned that interest you no longer have to pay as surely as getting a dividend on Coca-Cola.

Paid-for real estate will not bankrupt you. Paid-for real estate will not cause your expenses to exceed your income even if you get to the point that you have no income. Paid-for real estate is unaffected by the ups and downs of the market. Paid-for real estate can create income. Paid-for real estate can take care of you for the rest of your life.

Insurance

Buy insurance. Insure your health against unexpected medical expenses and catastrophic illness. Insure your business against liabilities that can take a lifetime of labor from you. Insure your assets from casualty. Insure your income in case you live long and insure your life because you will surely die and leave obligations to be paid.

Retirement

Retire now. Enjoy today. Play golf today. Travel today. Quilt today. Do not wait for someday because someday never comes. All we have for certain is today. Take it. Seize it. Make the decision to take a little of your retirement today and every day. And when you have made the decision to do these things, never retire. Super agents can work as long as they wish. Our profession has centenarians. Many agents work into their eighties and nineties. What better do you have to do than help people? When you are older and wiser your help has even greater value. Write out your bucket list and do number seven today. Put up your vision board and expect results sooner than later. Life is good and if you are a super agent, it is a super life.

Give

JoAnn has often said, "You can't give it away." In 2007 I had an opportunity to test her admonition. In August of that year the no-documentation loan disappeared and our industry began its greatest tumble in modern memory. Over the next 24 months, property values dropped by half and trillions of dollars in home equity vanished. Tragedy and loss seemed to surround us and I looked for every way to survive. Being superstitious, I began donating a small amount of money to various causes who sent us their appeals. Each week, as we paid the business invoices, I included one of these small checks for every five bills I paid. I was a voodoo priest incanting over the envelopes.

I don't expect you to become a believer. I can hardly explain it myself. But we survived 2008 and then 2009. One after the other, opportunities presented themselves at the last possible moment. We were, for want of any other word, lucky. I'm not saying you should make a donation and head for the closest Indian casino but a generous heart does experience good fortune.

My grandmother used to tell my mother that I should travel. I was only a child but a distant cousin had joined the Navy and seen the poverty in the world and returned with a new appreciation for his simple life in the dust bowl of Oklahoma. Today, we can sit in our living rooms as the miseries of the world are brought to us on television and the Internet. We don't even have to leave our shores. The needs in our own communities are laid bare in digital high definition. We all should be humbled like my cousin and those of us who have experienced good fortune have an obligation to help those in need.

Over the years JoAnn and I have built a house for Habitat for Humanity, made a dying child's wish come true, and, during the foreclosure crises, we helped make sure no pets were left behind in empty homes of broken dreams. In 2013, JoAnn and I went to lunch with Marlene Klotz-Collins, a member of the Salvation Army's national advisory board and an extraordinary human being. She told us about the Army's history and we related the reason for our donations over the years. I left out the part about voodoo incantations.

Back when we were in high school we knew a girl named Alice. She had moved away and found herself in an abusive marriage. One night she decided to run. She put her three small children in the back seat of her car and started for home, 1,500 miles away. She had no one to call. Her parents had not approved. She didn't know what she would face when she got there. She only knew she had to leave.

Alice got as far as Joplin, Missouri, where she put her last $2 in the gas tank. It wasn't enough to get her home. The children were hungry and she told the station attendant of her situation. He told her to go to the Salvation Army and gave her directions. It was past midnight and when she arrived a woman answered the bell. Within 15 minutes Alice was given $100, no questions asked. She fed her children, filled her tank, and made it home. Many who heard this story, including us, have donated that original $100 back to the Army many times since.

As we ate, the subject of the Christmas kettles came up and JoAnn told Marlene how we always put money in the kettle both when entering a store and when coming out. It was my job to have the cash at hand. One day as we arrived at Dillard's I found my pockets empty and JoAnn simply said, "I'll wait." She sat down on a bench and pointed to the ATM at the bank across the parking lot. Let me tell you, ATMs do not dispense one-dollar bills and I've never been without cash in my pockets at Christmas since.

Marlene loved that story and she told us that it was easy to get volunteers to ring the bells on the weekends but that on Wednesdays the Army had to pay minimum wage and transport workers to the kettles. For some, the earnings were a form of charity in itself but most were less enthusiastic and the Army often lost money on Wednesdays. When JoAnn heard this she volunteered us and then she volunteered the entire home-ownership industry. Real Estate Wednesdays were born.

In 2013 brokers, agents, title companies, lenders, and affiliates came together in Phoenix, Arizona, and manned more than 180 kettles on each of the three Wednesdays between Thanksgiving and New Year's. They raised over $117,000 and saved $85,000 in expenses for a $202,000 positive impact.

Give Back

Ours is a wonderful profession and we are all served by the National Association of Realtors. The NAR gives us a voice in Washington and provides education and ethical oversight to its members. Through state and local associations you have an opportunity to give back.

Our brokers do their best to provide educational opportunities to their agents, but when a super agent mentors a newbie the magic is made real.

So many organizations and home-tour groups need your participation and membership.

John F. Kennedy challenged us all when he said, "Ask not what your country can do for you, but what you can do for your country." As a super agent, change the words country for profession and make a difference.

Make yours a super life.

Chapter 23 Summary

Work

- Work less.
- Live more.
- Earn only to pay for the rest.

Family

- Family is for life.
- Forgive.
- Love anyway.

Health

- Value your health.
- Avoid stress.
- Think prevention.

Wealth

- Live within your means.
- Save on taxes but pay them.
- Credit is permission to owe money.

Investment

- Buy real estate.
- Pay off real estate.
- Paid-for real estate will take care of you.

Insurance

- Insure your health.
- Insure your wealth.
- Insure your life.

Retirement

- Live today.
- Someday never comes.
- Never retire.

Give

- You can't give it away.
- Make donations along with paying your bills.
- We have an obligation to help those less fortunate.

Give Back

- Support your local and national associations.
- Support your broker.
- Make a difference.

Doing the Most Good: The Salvation Army

The Salvation Army, which provides assistance to those in need 365 days a year, is often described as a "best-kept secret." Their work in disaster relief is particularly poignant. The Salvation Army was the first relief agency to reach Ground Zero on the morning of September 11, reporting within a half-hour following the first plane crash. They were given full control of the feeding operation at Ground Zero and for the nine months that followed, served 3.2 million meals with the assistance of 39,000 Salvation Army officers, volunteers, and staff. As always, they provided emotional and spiritual counseling and support to victims as well as rescue and recovery personnel. Whatever the disaster—floods, hurricanes, tidal waves, tornadoes—the Salvation Army is there within minutes and stays for as many months or years as necessary.

Founded in London in 1865 by a Methodist minister, William Booth, and his wife, Catherine, the Salvation Army is an international organization that meets the physical and spiritual needs of people in 125 countries around the world, without discrimination.

With nearly 7,700 centers of operation (corps) in the United States, the Salvation Army assists nearly 30 million individuals, or one person per second, nationwide throughout the year, almost 4.5 million of those during the holiday season alone.

Eighty-three percent of donations go directly to program funding to help people who need it most. In times of disaster, 100 percent of donations received go directly to the designated disaster.

The Salvation Army's services may vary from state to state. In Arizona's Valley of the Sun (greater Phoenix area), the Army provides the following programs, facilities, and services through 13 corps:

- Homeless shelter and regular feeding programs
- Emergency assistance (food, utilities, rent)
- Project HOPE (daily contact with homeless individuals on the streets)
- Substance abuse recovery (free six-month residential/work therapy)
- Domestic violence shelters
- Military assistance
- Low-income senior housing
- Senior recreation programs/facilities
- Variety of youth mentoring, tutoring, and academic programs
- Youth and adult sports programs
- Camp Ponderosa Ranch (Heber) for underprivileged youth and others
- Disaster services (food and shelter—100 percent of disaster donations go to the designated disaster)
- Thanksgiving and Christmas Day dinners (6,000 in 2013; 2,500 home-delivered)
- Christmas Angel (new toys for 50,000 Valley of the Sun children)
- Adopt-a-Family (350 families in 2013)

The red Christmas kettle debuted in San Francisco in 1891 in the guise of a crab pot. A depression had thrown many out of work, including hundreds of seamen and longshoremen. A Salvation Army officer put the pot on a wharf and collected enough coins to serve holiday dinners to those in need. By 1900, the program had spread nationwide.

In Phoenix, donations from the red kettles and year-end gifts from donors account for 60 percent of the funding required for the Army's year-round social programs.

The Salvation Army's Adult Rehabilitation Center, a free substance abuse program, is funded solely through donations received by and then sold through thrift/family stores.

For more information about the Salvation Army in your area, contact www.salvation armyusa.org or contact JoAnn Callaway at 480-596-5751.

B Real Estate Wednesdays

It began as many great things do, unexpectedly over a quiet lunch between friends. Super volunteer and member of the Salvation Army's National Advisory Board, Marlene Klotz-Collins, was welcoming Joseph and JoAnn Callaway to the organization's Phoenix Advisory Board. JoAnn told Marlene how dedicated she and Joseph were to the red kettles at Christmas. Marlene explained to JoAnn that Wednesdays were a challenge when getting volunteers. "The Army actually has to hire paid workers to ring bells at many of the kettle locations," Marlene said. JoAnn immediately volunteered herself and Joseph, and by dessert she had volunteered the whole home ownership industry.

After months of planning, more than 1,000 real estate agents, title company officers, lenders, and affiliates came together to ring the bells at more than 180 kettle locations throughout Maricopa County. Real Estate Wednesdays was born.

The effort has three goals:

1. To be a part of all that the Salvation Army does and to be part of a greater cause for good.
2. To elevate the public image and perception of our real estate industry as a cooperative and caring group.
3. To connect and reconnect with clients and the community we serve.

An unexpected difference is best summed up in an e-mail from Old Republic Title Officer Alison Hudgins: "I am so personally touched by my experience that I will never allow another Christmas to go by without ringing."

For 2013, Real Estate Wednesdays included the three Wednesdays between Thanksgiving and Christmas. In 2014, there will be four Wednesdays, including Christmas Eve.

The Salvation Army's support was amazing. They brought the kettles each morning and they picked them up each night. The first Wednesday went off without a single complaint. "It was such a blessing," says Marlene Klotz-Collins. "In addition to the more than $117,000 raised by the home ownership industry and the $85,000 in saved expenses, the awareness of the Army was heightened, companies and families began new traditions, and there was tremendous cost savings to the Army because it was an all-volunteer effort, executed in the classiest, most professional style possible."

For more information and a full list of this season's participants, visit the website and blog at www.RealEstateWednesdays.com.

It is our hope to volunteer the entire home ownership industry nationwide. If you would like more information or you would like to spearhead the effort in your area, please call JoAnn Callaway at 480-596-5751.

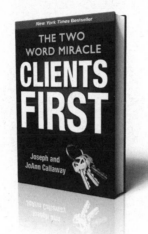

"A Clients First Company"

www.ThoseCallaways.com

Arizona's most trusted name in Real Estate
Serving Arizona since 1997
480-596-5751

"First, be a good agent"

www.SuperAgentBook.com

Follow Joseph and JoAnn's Appearance Calendar
Direct Order and Bulk Sales
Check Out Our Blog

About the Authors

Prior to writing their *New York Times* best seller *Clients First*, Those Callaways were the number one agents in Arizona by sales volume for more than a decade. First licensed in 1996, Those Callaways sold an unprecedented one billion dollars' worth of real estate, more than 4,000 homes, in just their first 10 years. Today, they are hard at work on their second billion and own Those Callaways Real Estate LLC, a boutique brokerage with 30 agents who work as a team to serve each client.

Clients First became a *New York Times* best seller in November 2012 and was the number one business book in *The Wall Street Journal*. Its message of honesty, competence, and care is being embraced daily by not only real estate agents, but practitioners in all industries.

Originally from Decatur, Illinois, Joseph and JoAnn have been Arizona residents since 1982. They live in Scottsdale, and JoAnn wishes it had a beach.

Index